EVALUATING EYEWITNESS IDENTIFICATION

BEST PRACTICES IN FORENSIC MENTAL HEALTH ASSESSMENT

Series Editors

Thomas Grisso, Alan M. Goldstein, and Kirk Heilbrun

Series Advisory Board

Paul Appelbaum, Richard Bonnie, and John Monahan

Titles in the Series

Foundations of Forensic Mental Health Assessment, *Kirk Heilbrun, Thomas Grisso, and Alan M. Goldstein*

Criminal Titles

Evaluation of Competence to Stand Trial, *Patricia A. Zapf and Ronald Roesch*

Evaluation of Criminal Responsibility, *Ira K. Packer*

Evaluation of Capacity to Confess, *Alan M. Goldstein and Naomi Goldstein*

Evaluation of Sexually Violent Predators, *Philip H. Witt and Mary Alice Conroy*

Evaluation for Risk of Violence in Adults, *Kirk Heilbrun*

Jury Selection, *Margaret Bull Kovera and Brian L. Cutler*

Evaluation for Capital Sentencing, *Mark D. Cunningham*

Eyewitness Identification, *Brian L. Cutler and Margaret Bull Kovera*

Civil Titles

Evaluation of Capacity to Consent to Treatment and Research, *Scott Y. H. Kim*

Evaluation for Guardianship, *Eric Y. Drogin and Curtis L. Barrett*

Evaluation for Personal Injury Claims, *Andrew W. Kane and Joel Dvoskin*

Evaluation for Civil Commitment, *Debra Pinals and Douglas Mossman*

Evaluation for Harassment and Discrimination Claims, *William Foote and Jane Goodman-Delahunty*

Evaluation of Workplace Disability, *Lisa D. Piechowski*

Juvenile and Family Titles

Evaluation for Child Custody, *Geri S.W. Fuhrmann*

Evaluation of Juveniles' Competence to Stand Trial, *Ivan Kruh and Thomas Grisso*

Evaluation for Risk of Violence in Juveniles, *Robert Hoge and D.A. Andrews*

Evaluation for Child Protection, *Karen S. Budd, Jennifer Clark, Mary Connell, and Kathryn Kuehnle*

Evaluation for Disposition and Transfer of Juvenile Offenders, *Randall T. Salekin*

EVALUATING EYEWITNESS IDENTIFICATION

BRIAN L. CUTLER

AND MARGARET BULL KOVERA

OXFORD
UNIVERSITY PRESS

2010

OXFORD
UNIVERSITY PRESS

Oxford University Press, Inc., publishes works that further
Oxford University's objective of excellence
in research, scholarship, and education.

Oxford New York
Auckland   Cape Town   Dar es Salaam   Hong Kong   Karachi
Kuala Lumpur   Madrid   Melbourne   Mexico City   Nairobi
New Delhi   Shanghai   Taipei Toronto

With offices in
Argentina   Austria   Brazil   Chile   Czech Republic   France   Greece
Guatemala   Hungary   Italy   Japan   Poland   Portugal   Singapore
South Korea   Switzerland   Thailand   Turkey   Ukraine   Vietnam

Copyright © 2010 by Oxford University Press, Inc.

Published by Oxford University Press, Inc.
198 Madison Avenue, New York, New York 10016

www.oup.com

Oxford is a registered trademark of Oxford University Press

Library of Congress Cataloging-in-Publication Data
Cutler, Brian L.
   Evaluating eyewitness identification / Brian L. Cutler, Margaret Bull
Kovera.
     p.   cm. — (Best practices in forensic mental health assessment)
Includes bibliographical references and index.
ISBN 978-0-19-537268-7
   1. Eyewitness identification—United States.   2. Forensic psychology—
United States.   I. Kovera, Margaret Bull, 1966–   II. Title.
KF9672.C8678 2010
345.73'066—dc22

                                                          2009040535

9 8 7 6 5 4 3 2 1

Printed in the United States of America
on acid-free paper

About Best Practices in Forensic Mental Health Assessment

The recent growth in the fields of forensic psychology and forensic psychiatry has created a need for this book series describing best practices in forensic mental health assessment (FMHA). Currently, forensic evaluations are conducted by mental health professionals for a variety of criminal, civil, and juvenile legal questions. The research foundation supporting these assessments has become broader and deeper in recent decades. Consensus has become clearer on the recognition of essential requirements for ethical and professional conduct. In the larger context of the current emphasis on "empirically supported" assessment and intervention in psychiatry and psychology, the specialization of FMHA has advanced sufficiently to justify a series devoted to best practices. Although this series focuses mainly on evaluations conducted by psychologists and psychiatrists, the fundamentals and principles offered also apply to evaluations conducted by clinical social workers, psychiatric nurses, and other mental health professionals.

This series describes "best practice" as empirically supported (when the relevant research is available), legally relevant, and consistent with the applicable ethical and professional standards. Authors of the books in this series identify the approaches that seem best, while incorporating what is practical and acknowledging that best practice represents a goal to which the forensic clinician should aspire, rather than a standard that can always be met. The American Academy of Forensic Psychology assisted the editors in enlisting the consultation of board-certified forensic psychologists specialized in each topic area. Board-certified forensic psychiatrists were also consultants on many of the volumes. Their comments on the manuscripts helped to ensure that the methods described in these volumes represent a generally accepted view of best practice.

The series' authors were selected for their specific expertise in a particular area. At the broadest level, however, certain general principles apply to all types of forensic evaluations. Rather than repeat those fundamental principles in every volume, the series offers them in the first volume, *Foundations of Forensic Mental Health Assessment*. Reading the first book, followed by a specific topical book, will provide the reader both the general principles that the specific topic shares with all forensic evaluations and those that are particular to the specific assessment question.

The specific topics of the 19 books were selected by the series editors as the most important and oft-considered areas of forensic assessment conducted by mental health professionals and behavioral scientists. Each of the 19 topical books is organized according to a common template. The authors address the applicable legal context, forensic mental health concepts, and empirical foundations and limits in the "Foundation" part of the book. They then describe preparation for the evaluation, data collection, data interpretation, and report writing and testimony in the "Application" part of the book. This creates a fairly uniform approach to considering these areas across different topics. All authors in this series have attempted to be as concise as possible in addressing best practice in their area. In addition, topical volumes feature elements to make them user-friendly in actual practice. These elements include boxes that highlight especially important information, relevant case law, best-practice guidelines, and cautions against common pitfalls. A glossary of key terms is also provided in each volume.

We hope the series will be useful for different groups of individuals. Practicing forensic clinicians will find succinct, current information relevant to their practice. Those who are in training to specialize in FMHA (whether in formal training or in the process of respecialization) should find helpful the combination of broadly applicable considerations presented in the first volume together with the more specific aspects of other volumes in the series. Those who teach and supervise trainees can offer these volumes as a guide for practices to which the trainee can aspire. Researchers and scholars interested in FMHA best practice may find researchable ideas, particularly on topics that have received insufficient research attention to date. Judges and attorneys with questions about FMHA best practice will find these books relevant and concise. Clinical and forensic administrators who run agencies, court clinics, and hospitals in which litigants are assessed may also use some of the books in this series to establish expectancies for evaluations performed by professionals in their agencies.

We also anticipate that the 19 specific books in this series will serve as reference works that help courts and attorneys evaluate the quality of forensic mental health professionals' evaluations. A word of caution is in order, however. These volumes focus on best practice, not what is minimally acceptable legally or ethically. Courts involved in malpractice litigation, or ethics committees or licensure boards considering complaints, should not expect that materials describing best practice easily or necessarily translate into the minimally acceptable professional conduct that is typically at issue in such proceedings.

This book addresses best practice standards in evaluating and testifying about the accuracy of eyewitness identification. Eyewitness testimony plays a critical role in criminal trials. Witnesses and victims of crimes are often called by prosecutors to the witness stand and, under oath, identify the defendant as the perpetrator of the crime. Such testimony carries significant weight for members of the jury and may be a major factor in contributing to a finding of guilt. However, numerous factors may distort eyewitness memories and make such testimony unreliable. Cutler and Kovera review the literature on eyewitness identification and discuss the role of forensic mental health professionals as expert witnesses on this topic. This volume addresses methods for evaluating eyewitness testimony, how experts can work with attorneys and what experts can and cannot testify to on this topic. Their book will serve as a guide for forensic mental health professional when conducting assessments that are legally relevant, consistent with professional ethics, empirically grounded, and how to present their findings in an objective and thorough fashion.

Alan M. Goldstein
Thomas Grisso
Kirk Heilbrun

Acknowledgments

We wish to thank Craig and Hope Kovera and Karin, Penelope, Dennis, and Alison Cutler for their support and patience as we advanced this work from inception to the final pages.

We wish to thank Alan Goldstein, Tom Grisso, and Kirk Heilbrun for the opportunity to contribute to this impressive series and for their guidance. We thank Kimberly Ackerson for her constructive feedback on an earlier version of this manuscript.

We dedicate this book to Steve Penrod, research mentor to both authors and eyewitness expert in every sense.

Contents

FOUNDATION

The Legal Context 1

E yewitnesses play a prominent role in many criminal cases. By providing descriptions of crimes and perpetrators, they may aid police investigators in the apprehension of criminal suspects. As criminal investigations proceed, detectives conduct subsequent interviews with eyewitnesses and eyewitnesses may identify crime perpetrators from lineups or photoarrays. If a case goes to trial, eyewitnesses may be called upon to recount the crime details and identify the crime perpetrator in court. *Eyewitness testimony* has proven to be highly influential with juries (Cutler & Penrod, 1995), and in some types of cases (e.g., robberies), it is often the only evidence linking the defendant with the crime.

The willingness of eyewitnesses to aid in the apprehension, prosecution, and adjudication of criminal offenders is to be lauded. Eyewitnesses are often innocent bystanders or victims of the crimes. They typically have nothing to gain by serving as witnesses beyond the personal satisfaction of aiding justice. They may perceive risk to themselves and their families by accusing members of their communities of serious criminal activity. In short, eyewitnesses provide an important service to the criminal justice system with little personal gain and much to lose. It is no wonder that some eyewitnesses prefer not to get involved in criminal investigations.

Does the involvement of eyewitnesses in the criminal justice system improve the quality of justice dispensed by our legal system? How accurate are eyewitnesses? To what extent can we rely on eyewitnesses to recall crime details and identify crime perpetrators accurately? The human ability to recall details of events and recognize people from the past is impressive. Indeed, such skills are

INFO

Memory is susceptible to error. Crimes often take place under circumstances that facilitate memory errors. The nature of the crime itself can directly affect memory. Exposure to the crime perpetrator might be very brief and may take place under stressful conditions. The perpetrator may be from a racial group that is different from that of the witness and with which the witness has little personal experience. Perpetrators may threaten witnesses with a weapon, causing them to fear for their personal safety, even fearing that the perpetrator may intend to fatally harm them. It may take the police many months to locate a suspect to present to a witness in a lineup or photoarray. Such conditions may challenge eyewitnesses' ability to recognize a crime perpetrator who is a complete stranger to them. Because of the unique and difficult circumstances in which crimes occur, eyewitnesses sometimes make mistakes and they may never become aware that they have made a mistake.

necessary for day-to-day living. With reasonable ease we can recall our activities of the day, and we routinely and accurately recognize our friends and relatives. Although our memory normally serves us well, it is far from perfect and can be quite fragile in certain circumstances.

Mistakes of Eyewitnesses

How do we know that eyewitnesses make mistakes? Several sources of evidence can be brought to bear on this question. First, there is a substantial body of literature on *erroneous conviction*. There are a growing number of identified cases in which citizens have been convicted of serious crimes, imprisoned—sometimes for many years—and later found to be innocent of the crimes for which they were convicted and sentenced. In many such cases, eyewitness identification is the only evidence linking the defendant to the crime. Among the more recent and compelling studies of erroneous conviction is the ongoing work of the Innocence Project, founded by attorney Barry Scheck and his colleagues. The aim of the Innocence Project is to use DNA evidence to uncover erroneous convictions and exonerate the wrongfully convicted. Thus far their efforts have led to the exoneration of over 200 such individuals throughout the United States (see www.innocenceproject.com). The factors leading to erroneous conviction were examined by the Innocence Project and in studies on erroneous conviction (e.g., Borchard, 1932; Frank & Frank, 1957; Garrett, 2008; Huff, 1987). Consistently, authors of these studies found *mistaken identification* to be the most common feature of erroneous conviction cases.

1
chapter

INFO

Mistaken identification is commonly a factor in erroneous conviction. Well-intentioned eyewitnesses mistakenly identified innocent suspects as crime perpetrators in the vast majority of these cases. Even identification of the same person by multiple witnesses does not guarantee that the witnesses have accurately identified the perpetrator. In a number of cases, multiple eyewitnesses mistakenly identified the same innocent suspects. Laboratory, field, and archival research on eyewitness memory also suggests that eyewitnesses are capable of making mistakes and that mistaken identifications are very common. Mistaken identifications can also occur in laboratory studies, which typically consist of an environment or situation that is seemingly less stressful than what an eyewitness would experience during an actual crime situation. Rates of false identification in laboratory research vary from close to 0% to close to 100%, depending on the specific conditions associated with the study. Although it is difficult—if not impossible—to calculate the rate of mistaken identifications in lineups conducted in the course of investigating actual crimes, studies reveal that witnesses of real crimes mistakenly identify *fillers* (i.e., known innocents) in the lineup in substantial numbers. Behrman and Davey's (2001) review of police records for 271 cases in Sacramento, California, revealed that 24% of witnesses in these cases identified a known innocent lineup member. An analysis of identification decisions in 280 lineups in Hennepin County, Minnesota, revealed a filler identification rate of 11% (Klobuchar, Steblay, & Caligiuri, 2006). If some witnesses in real cases are mistakenly identifying innocent fillers, it stands to reason that some witnesses are also mistakenly identifying innocent suspects.

Safeguards to Erroneous Conviction

That mistaken eyewitness identifications occur should not *necessarily* be a problem for the criminal justice system. False identifications may on occasion lead to false arrests, false indictments, or trials with innocent defendants, but other procedural safeguards exist to protect defendants from erroneous conviction resulting from mistaken eyewitness identification. These safeguards include

- the representation of the defendant by an attorney at lineups;
- pretrial motions to have identification testimony based on the use of unduly suggestive procedures suppressed;
- the opportunity to question prospective jurors during jury selection procedures (i.e., *voir dire*) about their willingness to scrutinize eyewitness identification testimony and to exclude from jury service those who express an unwillingness or inability to perform this function;
- the opportunity to cross-examine eyewitnesses thoroughly at trial; and
- instructions to the jury from the judge that provide guidance about how to evaluate the reliability of eyewitness testimony.

Each of these safeguards, however, has been found lacking for both conceptual and empirical reasons (Van Wallendael et al., 2007). Defense attorneys are rarely present at preindictment identification procedures, and empirical evidence suggests that they may miss some forms of procedural bias like biased instructions even if they were present (Stinson, Devenport, Cutler, & Kravitz, 1996). If attorneys have difficulty identifying procedural bias then it is unlikely that they will be able to effectively argue about this bias in pretrial motions to suppress the identification evidence. It appears as if judges are somewhat better at identifying procedural biases than are attorneys but they misunderstand which method of lineup presentation produces more reliable identifications (Stinson, Devenport, Cutler, & Kravitz, 1997). Trial procedures such as *cross-examination* that are intended to educate jurors about the potential unreliability of evidence appear to have limited effectiveness (Devenport, Stinson, Cutler, & Kravitz, 2002). The limited effectiveness of cross-examination is due to the insensitivity of attorneys (who ask the questions) and jurors (who evaluate the testimony) to the factors known from scientific research to influence identification accuracy.

Expert Testimony

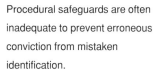

Expert testimony on eyewitness memory differs in significant ways from expert testimony commonly provided by psychologists. Frequently, when psychologists testify as expert witnesses, their testimony is based on the evaluation of a defendant or litigant. For example, experts may offer opinions as to whether a defendant is competent to stand trial or to waive rights (e.g., *Miranda* rights). The expert's testimony is based on an evaluation of the individual, typically a formal forensic mental heath assessment. The expert may have interviewed the individual, studied the individual's medical history, and performed psychological tests on the individual. The expert then reports the results of the assessment and may provide a recommendation to the court during expert testimony. Monahan and Walker (1986) refer to this form of expert testimony as "social fact" evidence. The expert's testimony has a direct bearing on a fact to be adjudicated, such as whether a defendant is competent to stand trial.

INFO

Procedural safeguards are often inadequate to prevent erroneous conviction from mistaken identification.

Although these safeguards probably prevent some mistaken identifications from resulting in erroneous convictions, they are not fully effective (as evidenced by the studies showing that mistaken identification is the most common feature of the DNA exoneration cases). Erroneous convictions that are at least partly the result of mistaken identification continue to accumulate and to be documented by the Innocence Project. The fallibility of safeguards designed to protect defendants from erroneous conviction resulting from mistaken identification has led to the development of a relatively new safeguard, *expert testimony about the psychology of eyewitness memory* (henceforth abbreviated as "expert testimony" unless otherwise noted).

The eyewitness expert, however, does not perform an evaluation of the witness or offer any opinion or recommendation about the witness. Rather, the eyewitness expert testifies in general terms about the psychological processes underlying human memory and about the factors associated with the crime and identification that have been shown by the research to influence the likelihood of a false identification. In Monahan and Walker's (1986) scheme, expert testimony is an example of "social framework" testimony. The issue in dispute—the accuracy of the identification—is an instance to which a general theory or research finding applies. The expert, therefore, provides the framework, based on the current research on eyewitness memory, for evaluating the identification. The expert, for example, might testify that cross-race recognitions and identifications made by witnesses who were traumatized by a violent crime are less likely to be correct than same-race identifications and identifications made after innocuous events. The expert might also testify about how certain lineup procedures increase the likelihood of false identification. The expert does not, however, offer an opinion, actual or hypothetical, about the accuracy of eyewitness testimony in the case. Determining the accuracy of eyewitness testimony is clearly the province of the jury. Expert testimony is typically proffered by the defense in criminal cases in which eyewitness identification (or eyewitness recall) is being challenged.

Eyewitness Research

Elizabeth Loftus and Robert Buckhout are among the matriarchs and patriarchs in the field of eyewitness research and were among the first scholars to offer expert testimony on this topic. The research base that forms the foundation for eyewitness memory is extensive. A vast scientific literature has developed since the 1970s. The topics of this research include the reliability of eyewitness identification, factors affecting the reliability of eyewitness identification, methods of improving eyewitness identification accuracy, and the effectiveness of safeguards designed to protect defendants from erroneous conviction resulting from mistaken eyewitness identification. Apart from eyewitness identification, there are research literatures on the factors affecting and the methods of improving eyewitness recall, the accuracy of children's memories, and the factors affecting the development of false memories. Research on eyewitness memory is regularly published in reputable scientific journals such as *Law and Human Behavior*, *Applied Cognitive Psychology*, *Journal of Applied Social Psychology*, *Journal of Experimental Psychology: Applied; Psychology, Public Policy, & Law*; and *Psychology, Crime & the Law*. There are dozens of books devoted to the topic of eyewitness memory, including an impressive, recently published two-volume *Handbook of Eyewitness Testimony* (Lindsay, Ross, Read, & Toglia, 2007). Eyewitness research is a common topic at meetings of the American Psychology-Law Society and the Society of Applied Research on Memory and Cognition, and at other conferences devoted to research at the intersection of psychology and law, and it is discussed in many textbooks on General Psychology, Cognitive Psychology, Human Memory, and Social Psychology.

The Experts

Who are the experts who offer testimony about eyewitness identification? Kassin and his colleagues have tracked the incidences of expert testimony in two studies. In their first study (Kassin, Ellsworth & Smith, 1989), 119 eyewitness experts (i.e., scholars who published on the topic of eyewitness memory) were surveyed about their experiences as expert witnesses, 63 of whom provided survey responses. Of the 63 respondents, 48 (76%) were members of the American Psychology-Law Society, Division 41, of the American Psychological Association (APA). About half of the respondents (49%) were social or personality psychologists, 27%

were cognitive psychologists, 14% were clinical psychologists, and the remaining 8% were from other areas of the discipline. Three-quarters of the experts reported serving as author or coauthor of at least one publication on eyewitness memory, and the mean number of relevant publications authored by the respondents was 6.35.

How often do they testify? What was their level of involvement in actual cases? These experts were asked to testify in 1,268 cases, and they agreed to testify in 935 cases (74%). However, they actually testified in 478 cases, which represents 51% of the cases in which they agreed to testify and 38% of the cases in which they were asked to testify. About half (54%) testified in court at least once. In most (76%) of the 478 cases in which the experts testified, the testimony was proffered by the defense in a criminal case, followed by the plaintiff in a civil case (11%), the defense in a civil case (6%), and the prosecution in a criminal case (6%).

Kassin, Tubb, Hosch, and Memon (2001) published a follow-up study to this initial survey of eyewitness experts. This study was very similar to the first, although it was conducted more than a decade later and followed the publication of some authoritative research on eyewitness memory. They identified 197 experts, of whom 65 provided survey responses. There were some differences in respondent profiles from the 1989 study. About half (52%) of the experts were cognitive psychologists, 26% were social or personality psychologists, 9% were developmental psychologists, 5% were clinical or counseling psychologists, and the remainder (6%) were from more than one subdiscipline of psychology. The main difference seems to be the relative balance of cognitive and social psychologists in the samples, with cognitive psychologists being better represented and social psychologists less well-represented in the more recent study. The qualifications of the experts differed between the two studies. The experts in the 2001 study had more publications. They averaged 2 books, 6.5 chapters, and 13 journal articles about eyewitness memory.

As in the 1989 study, the experts were much more likely to testify in criminal cases than in civil cases and were proffered far more often by the defense in criminal cases. Requests from criminal defense attorneys accounted for 89% of all requests for testimony. The most striking difference between the 1989 and 2001 studies, however, is the dramatic increase in testimony. In the 2001 study, the experts reported being asked to testify in 3,370 instances, an increase of 266%. They agreed to testify in 1,373 cases, i.e., in 41% of the cases in which they were asked to testify, an increase of 47% over the 1989 figure. They actually testified in 960 cases, representing 28% of the cases in which they were asked and 70% of the cases in which they agreed to testify. Thus, this sample of experts reported testifying twice as often as the sample of experts from the 1989 study. Hence, the practice of providing expert testimony on the psychology of eyewitness memory (henceforth referred to as "expert testimony") began to emerge as the research literature on eyewitness memory began to mature.

Legal Standards for Expert Testimony

The legal standards governing admissibility of expert testimony on eyewitness memory are, of course, the same legal standards that govern expert testimony generally. The Federal Rules of Evidence (1975) consider an individual to be qualified as an expert if she is able to assist the trier of fact. The level of qualifications required to be admitted as an expert varies as a function of the demands of the testimony to be offered by the expert (Faigman, 2008). As noted above, many eyewitness experts possess doctoral degrees and have published extensively on the topic of eyewitness memory.

Several standards have governed the admissibility of expert testimony in U.S. courts, beginning with the *Frye* test (*Frye v. United States*, 1923), the Federal Rules of Evidence (1975), and a series of cases in the 1990s (*Daubert v. Merrell Dow Pharmaceuticals*, 1993;

CASE LAW

Frye v. United States (1923)

● established the *Frye* test, in which admissibility of expert testimony is dependent on the use of methods generally accepted by the relevant scientific community

● continues to be the legal standard for admissibility in some states (e.g., California, Florida, New York)

General Electric Co. v. Joiner, 1997; *Kumho Tire Company v. Carmichael*, 1999). The *Frye* test stated that the methods used by the expert must be generally accepted in the relevant scientific community. The *Frye* rule governed admissibility decisions in federal and state courts for 50 years and continues to be the legal standard for admissibility in some states (e.g., California, Florida, New York). In the mid-1970s, the Federal Rules of Evidence (1975) were adopted and included a rule that specifically governed the admissibility of expert testimony (Rule 702). Rule 702 stated that

> If scientific, technical, or other specialized knowledge will assist the trier of fact to understand the evidence or to determine a fact in issue, a witness qualified as an expert by knowledge, skill, experience, training, or education, may testify thereto in the form of an opinion or otherwise. (FRE, 1975, p. 14)

Although these new rules were binding only in federal courts, many state courts also adopted these evidentiary rules, either completely or with some modification, as well. This standard of admissibility appeared quite different from the earlier Frye test and arguments regarding which standard should prevail began appearing in the courts.

These arguments were finally resolved, at least for the federal courts, when the U.S. Supreme Court issued its decision in *Daubert v. Merrell Dow Pharmaceuticals, Inc.* (1993). In its decision, the Supreme Court developed a two-pronged test for admissibility. Consistent with Federal Rule 402, the first prong required that the expert testimony be relevant to an issue to be decided in the case. The second prong required that the evidence about which the expert proposes to testify be reliable. Essentially, this decision set forth the requirement that judges assess the scientific validity of the

CASE LAW

Daubert v. Merrell Dow Pharmaceuticals, Inc. (1993) established a two-pronged test for admissibility

1. expert testimony must be relevant to a debated issue in the case
2. the evidence presented by the expert witness must be reliable by scientific standards

methods used to generate the evidence to be presented when determining whether to admit proffered expert testimony.

The Court further suggested several criteria for determining the reliability of the methodology underlying the evidence to be presented:

- whether the theory relied on by the expert and the hypotheses being tested in the research were falsifiable;
- whether the expert evidence had been subjected to peer review;
- whether there is a known error rate associated with the expert evidence; and
- whether the evidence is generally accepted in the relevant scientific community.

In the *Joiner* decision, the U.S. Supreme Court affirmed the trial court's role as the gatekeeper, requiring judges to evaluate the reliability of the expert's methods and not abdicate their responsibility by appealing to a liberal interpretation of the Federal Rules of Evidence (Copple, Torkildson, & Kovera, 2008). In the *Kumho* case, the U.S. Supreme Court ruled that the *Daubert* test, designed to determine the admissibility of scientific testimony, should apply to nonscientific expert testimony as well. Given that the psychology of eyewitness memory is based on a foundation of research that relies upon the scientific method, we would argue that the *Daubert* standard clearly should be the relevant standard for judging the admissibility of expert testimony on eyewitness reliability. However, there are legal debates about whether psychology is a science. Although we believe there should be no question that the psychology of eyewitness memory is scientific, *Kumho* rendered the question moot as it extended the *Daubert* admissibility standard to all expert evidence.

As applied to expert testimony on eyewitness memory, the defense attorney, if practicing in a *Frye* state, must establish that the methodology and/or the findings of the proffered research are generally accepted in the field. We typically take this to mean that the eyewitness research to be summarized by the expert must be generally accepted in the field. In federal courts and state courts that have adopted the federal *Daubert* test, the defense attorney proffering expert testimony must establish that eyewitness research is based on reliable scientific methods. General acceptance of eyewitness research is one of many factors that may be given consideration in the *Daubert* test.

Denial of Expert Testimony

As discussed above, the Kassin et al. survey studies demonstrate that expert testimony occurs with increasing frequency. This is particularly true in states with case law that is favorable to expert testimony on eyewitness memory. In other states, however, case law is less favorable to expert testimony, and getting expert testimony admitted is a significant challenge. Expert testimony may be denied on several grounds. Perhaps the most common reason for refusing to admit expert testimony is the belief that the expert's testimony is within the ken of the jury and therefore not helpful (Schmechel, O'Toole, Easterly, & Loftus, 2006). Other reasons for refusing to admit expert testimony include the belief that the research is not scientifically reliable and the belief that the expert testimony will prejudice the jury. The validity of these beliefs is questionable, as we explain in chapter 3.

Legal Procedures

The legal procedures for expert testimony on eyewitness memory follow a familiar pattern (Figure 1.1). An expert's role in the case begins when an attorney with a case involving identification evidence makes initial contact with the eyewitness expert. This initial consultation usually consists of the attorney describing the facts of the case, an identification of topics, if any, about which the expert might testify, and a discussion of the expert's availability and fees. If an agreement is reached between the attorney and the expert, the attorney will provide the expert with any relevant discovery materials. After the expert reviews the discovery, there will likely be further consultation between the attorney and the expert. An expert retained early in the investigation may have a role in guiding discovery, suggesting documents

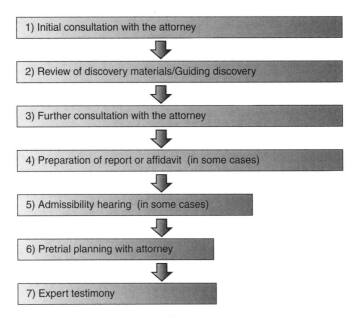

Figure 1.1 Typical pattern of legal procedures.

that might be obtained from the other side or information that might be gathered that would be relevant to the expert's opinion. In cases that move forward to trial, the expert may be asked to prepare a report or affidavit for distribution to the opposing attorney and judge. In some cases, the opposing attorney may wish to depose the expert before the trial. The attorney and expert must then work together to prepare for an admissibility hearing (in some cases) and for testimony before the jury if the expert is allowed to testify at trial. This collaboration involves careful planning of the *direct examinations* and *redirect examinations*.

Key Concepts in Eyewitness Identification | 2

I n this chapter we introduce key concepts that are necessary for understanding the research foundation underlying expert testimony. The actual research on the effects of witnessing conditions and identification procedures on eyewitness memory is reviewed in chapter 3.

Accuracy of Eyewitness Identification

The first key concept we address is identification accuracy. In order to understand how accuracy is defined, we must consider how lineups and photoarrays are composed and the types of judgments witnesses make in identification tasks. The purpose of an identification task is to assess whether the witness remembers the suspect. Although sometimes this goal is achieved by showing a witness a single suspect at the crime scene shortly after the crime occurred (referred to as a showup), this procedure provides no safeguards against witness guessing or faulty memory and can often be unduly suggestive (e.g., the suspect is in the back of the police car or standing by the car in handcuffs). Thus, when witnesses positively identify a suspect from a showup it is unclear whether the witness has an accurate memory of the perpetrator of the crime or whether the witness has made an inaccurate "guess" that the suspect is the perpetrator.

Similarly, a lineup consisting of members who are all suspects in the crime presents problems for the interpretation of witnesses' positive identifications. If witnesses positively identify any of the lineup members in this identification task, the identified lineup member is likely to be charged with and prosecuted for the crime in question. Again, this type of task does not provide a safeguard against witness guessing or poor memory because any lineup member chosen from an all-suspect lineup will likely become a defendant in short order.

Because of the problems of interpreting positive identifications from all-suspect lineups, it is commonly understood that a lineup should contain no more than one actual suspect. The suspect should be placed in the lineup together with some number of known innocent people. These known innocents are referred to as "fillers" or "foils." The purpose of fillers and other features of lineups are discussed below under "suspect bias factors." At this point, it is sufficient to understand that a lineup should consist of only one suspect and a set of fillers. The suspect might or might not be the perpetrator of the crime in question.

When an eyewitness is asked to identify a perpetrator from a lineup, several outcomes are possible. The eyewitness might identify a lineup member as the perpetrator ("that's him!"), indicate that the perpetrator is not among the lineup members ("she's not there"), or provide an ambiguous response (e.g., "I can't tell," "could be numbers 2 or 3," "looks like number 6 but I'm not sure"). In eyewitness research, we tend to focus on positive identifications ("that's him!") and rejections ("she's not there"). Positive identifications can further be divided into two types: identifications of suspects or identifications of fillers. When we recognize that there are two types of judgments (positive identifications and rejections), two types of positive identifications (suspect or a filler), and two types of suspects (innocent or guilty), we can create categories of accurate and inaccurate decisions (see Table 2.1).

Research on eyewitness identification typically distinguishes between correct identifications, false identifications, correct and incorrect rejections, and filler identifications as separate outcomes. The researchers are able to make this distinction because they rely

Table 2.1 Categories of Accurate and Inaccurate Eyewitness Identification Decisions

	Decision Type		
	Suspect ID	**Filler ID**	**Rejection**
Guilty suspect	Correct ID	Incorrect filler ID	Incorrect rejection
Innocent suspect	False ID	Incorrect filler ID	Correct rejection

heavily on crime simulation methodology, whereby eyewitnesses are exposed to simulated crimes and are later shown photoarrays. One of the main benefits of crime simulation research is that the investigator knows for certain which lineup member is the perpetrator and therefore knows whether a suspect identification is correct or mistaken and whether a rejection of the lineup represents an accurate decision that the perpetrator is not present or a missed identification of the perpetrator. Typically, the experimenter creates at least two types of lineups: *perpetrator-present* and *perpetrator-absent lineups.* Perpetrator-present lineups contain the perpetrator and a set of fillers. These lineups represent the situation in which the suspect is guilty. Perpetrator-absent lineups contain a person who resembles but is not the perpetrator and a set of fillers. These lineups represent the situation in which the suspect is innocent. Crime simulation methodology has both benefits and drawbacks, as will be discussed in chapter 3 (see section on limits), but an important benefit is the ability to distinguish, with certainty, accurate from inaccurate identifications and the various types of accurate and inaccurate identifications.

General Impairment Factors

General impairment factors are factors associated with the conditions under which a crime was witnessed and that affect the accuracy of eyewitness identification. Thus, they are called general impairment factors because their presence generally impairs the accuracy of eyewitness identification. Some of these factors are characteristics of the witness (e.g., the witness's race), some are characteristics of the perpetrators (e.g., whether the perpetrator was wearing a disguise), and some are situational factors (e.g., the stressfulness of the situation, whether there was a weapon present). These factors are also called *estimator variables* (Wells, 1978) because the presence of these factors allows for the estimation, in a very general manner, of the accuracy of an identification made by a witness under a particular set of witnessing conditions.

Identification Tests

Identification tests are the procedures used by the police that allow eyewitnesses to identify a suspect as the perpetrator of the crime that they witnessed. We call these procedures "tests" because they should be thought of as falling within the same category as other forensic identification tests. What is being tested in an identification test is the hypothesis that the suspect is the perpetrator. A positive identification of the suspect by the witness can be thought of as evidence supporting the hypothesis that the suspect is the perpetrator. A lineup rejection may be thought of as evidence against the hypothesis that the suspect is the perpetrator. In this context, a filler identification represents evidence against the hypothesis that the suspect is the perpetrator. There are two important concepts in this analysis: the nature of the hypothesis and the nature of the conclusions.

Nature of the Hypothesis

The hypothesis is so important that it deserves repetition: An identification test tests the hypothesis that the suspect is the perpetrator. When asked what a lineup tests, many investigators and lawyers will reply that the lineup tests whether the witness can identify the suspect. In the authors' experiences, this incorrect answer is given more commonly than the correct answer, and it is not a trick question. The failings of a test of whether the witness can identify the suspect should be obvious. First, such a test assumes that the suspect is the perpetrator. If it were factually known that the suspect is the perpetrator, there would be no need for an identification test. Second, the misguided hypothesis makes the test about the witness rather than the suspect. The implication of such a test is that a witness who identifies the suspect is a good witness, and a witness who fails to identify the suspect (i.e., fails the test) is not a good witness. In other words, when testing the hypothesis of whether the witness can identify the suspect, lineup rejections or filler identifications suggest that the witnesses' memory is imperfect and their failure to identify the suspect is nondiagnostic of whether the suspect is the perpetrator—rather than provide evidence that the suspect is not the perpetrator. These conclusions say nothing about the culpability of the suspect because the suspect is *presumed* to be the perpetrator.

INFO

An identification test tests the hypothesis that the suspect is the perpetrator. It should *not* be thought of as a test of whether the witness can correctly identify the suspect.

Nature of the Conclusion

Under the theory that the purpose of the identification test is to test the hypothesis that the suspect is the perpetrator, an identification of the suspect supports the hypothesis, whereas filler identifications or rejections do not support the hypothesis. The key distinction here is that we did not use the words "prove" or "disprove." We do not use these words because identification tests are imperfect. An understanding of the limitations of identification tests is critical for understanding the following description of *suspect bias factors* and for developing expert testimony.

Limitations of Identification Tests

The fundamental limitation of identification tests is that there are multiple reasons for which a witness might positively identify a suspect. One reason is the most obvious: witnesses might identify a suspect as the perpetrator because they recognize the suspect as the perpetrator based on their memory of the crime scene. Witnesses, however, might identify a suspect for a range of other reasons. Witnesses who are motivated to make a positive identification might guess who the suspect is and offer the guess as a positive identification. Likewise, witnesses who are motivated to make a positive identification might identify the suspect through the process of deduction. If, for example, the suspect stands out in some way in the identification test (e.g., the suspect is the only person who matches the witness's description of the perpetrator), a witness might deduce that this individual is the suspect and offer this deduction as a positive identification. Yet another possibility is that advertent or inadvertent influence by the investigator conducting the identification test may cause the witness to identify a suspect. Through subtle or nonsubtle cues, the investigator might convey to the witness that a particular lineup member (e.g., #4) is the suspect.

These explanations for suspect identifications vary with respect to the degree to which they implicate a suspect in the crime. An identification based on the witness's memory of the perpetrator is more diagnostic of the suspect's guilt than is an identification based on guessing, deduction, or investigator influence. How can one tell whether a suspect identification is based on recognition of the perpetrator from memory, guessing, deduction, or investigator influence? In the field, one cannot tell by the outcome of the identification test, particularly when the only record of the identification that goes forward is the witness's decision. One also cannot rely on witnesses to explain the basis of their identifications, for witnesses are not always privy to the factors that influence their decisions. In other words, witnesses may be influenced by the investigator conducting the lineup but may not realize it (Greathouse & Kovera, 2009). Also, witnesses who guess in order to be cooperative may not want to admit or may not be aware that they are guessing.

Structure of Identification Tests

The identification test must be structured in such a way as to increase the likelihood that the suspect identification is due to the witness's recollection of the perpetrator; also, it should minimize the likelihood that the identification is due to guessing, deduction, or investigator influence. Consider a simple example. Suppose an investigator has a photo of a suspect and wants to test his hypothesis that the suspect is the perpetrator using two witnesses, Harry and Hermione. Harry is shown the photo of the suspect and is asked whether the suspect is the person who committed the crime. Hermione is shown a set of 10 photos that includes the suspect's photo and 9 other photos that generally match Hermione's description of the perpetrator. Hermione is asked whether the perpetrator's photo is in the set of 10 photos and, if so, which photo is of the perpetrator. All other things being equal, the identification test given to Hermione is better than the one given to Harry for the following reasons. If Harry identifies the suspect's photo as that of the perpetrator, it is very difficult to know whether Harry's identification is based on his memory of the perpetrator or due to guessing or deduction. Guessing and deduction can easily explain Harry's positive identification because he was presented with only one photo. In Harry's identification test, the suspect's identity is obvious.

In contrast, if Hermione identifies the suspect's photo, it is more difficult (than in Harry's case) to conclude that she guessed which photo is of the suspect because she was shown 10 photos. Further, it is more difficult (than in Harry's case) to conclude that she deduced which photo is the photo of the suspect because all 10 photos matched the description of the perpetrator. She should not have been able to "rule out" any of the 10 photos on the basis of their descriptions, and the suspect's photo should not have stood out relative to the other photos. Thus, the structure of the identification test is the key to ruling out alternative explanations for positive identifications. Even under the best of circumstances, however, identification tests are still not perfect (nor are other forensic identification tests) and cannot prove the guilt or innocence of a suspect.

Types of Identification Tests

There are several types of identification tests that crime investigators rely upon for collecting eyewitness identification evidence.

Mugshot identifications involve providing the witnesses with books or stacks of photos of possible suspects. This is an exploratory procedure designed to generate leads rather than a confirmatory procedure designed to test whether a suspect is a perpetrator. As such, we do not focus on mugshot identifications in this volume. *Showups* involve the presentation of a single suspect to a witness for identification. Showups typically take place very soon after a crime, and the suspect is physically present, although occasionally a witness is presented with a photo of a suspect for identification (i.e., without fillers). *Photoarrays* refer to identification tests in which the witness is shown a set of photos containing a suspect's photo. *Live lineups* involve having the witness view a set of physically present individuals including a suspect.

In most jurisdictions, showups and photoarrays are more common methods of identification than are live lineups. Research on eyewitness identification is most likely to use photoarrays as the identification task. The principles associated with the construction and presentation of photoarrays and live lineups are very similar. There has been no research documenting differences in how lineup construction and presentation methods differentially affect live lineups and photoarrays. Accordingly, we do not distinguish between these methods in our review of suspect bias factors or in expert testimony. Unless we note otherwise, the research applying to photoarrays applies similarly to live lineups.

Suspect Bias Factors

Suspect bias factors refer to aspects of the identification test that bias the witness toward identifying the suspect regardless of whether the suspect is innocent or guilty. Suspect bias factors include the use of fillers in an identification test, the composition of the photoarray, and the procedures for conducting the photoarray. For example, photoarrays can be composed in such a way that only the photo of the suspect resembles the witness's description of the photoarray, and this biased composition of the lineup increases the likelihood that the witness will identify the suspect's photo regardless of whether the suspect is the perpetrator. As another example, biased instructions that imply the perpetrator is in the lineup can increase the likelihood that the witness identifies a suspect. In chapter 3, we review the research on suspect bias factors.

2
chapter

Postdictors of Identification Accuracy

Postdictors of identification accuracy are variables that are sometimes used to evaluate the accuracy of eyewitness identification but do not fall under the categories of general impairment and suspect bias factors. Examples of postdictors include the confidence of the eyewitness and the accuracy or consistency of eyewitness recall of crime details. They are called postdictors because these factors are used to try to gauge the accuracy of eyewitness identification after it has been made. Research on postdictors is reviewed in chapter 3.

Admissibility Concepts

State and federal courts differ with respect to their receptivity to expert testimony, as discussed in chapter 1. Some of the reasons cited for not admitting expert testimony have underlying behavioral assumptions. Researchers have conducted research on these behavioral assumptions, thus creating a body of scholarship directly addressing the validity of the rationales underlying admissibility decisions. This research as it relates to the admissibility of expert testimony on eyewitness reliability is reviewed in chapter 3.

One basis for challenging expert testimony is that the research about which the expert proposes to testify is that the testimony is not generally accepted within the scientific community, the *Frye* test, which we discussed previously. The research addressing the

INFO

Admissibility concepts include the following:

- general acceptance
- juror common understanding
- prejudicial impact versus probative value
- juror confusion

question of whether expert testimony is generally accepted within the scientific community is reviewed below. Another basis for challenging expert testimony is that the research is within the ken of the average juror, a concept drawn from the Federal Rules of Evidence. In other words, many judges conclude that jurors know how to evaluate eyewitnesses and do not need help from experts. But do jurors actually know how to evaluate eyewitness identifications? The research addressing this question is reviewed in chapter 3. Other reasons for excluding expert testimony include the belief that the prejudicial impact of expert testimony will outweigh its probative value or that the expert testimony will confuse the jury. What impact does expert testimony actually have on jurors? Research addressing this question is reviewed in chapter 3 as well.

Empirical Foundations and Limits | 3

T his chapter is divided into two sections. The first provides an overview of the research methods that have been used in research on eyewitness identification. The second section summarizes the research on general impairment factors, suspect bias factors, postdictors, and issues related to the admissibility of eyewitness's expert testimony.

Research Methods

Research on eyewitness identification uses the well-established methodology that is a part of scientific psychology. This research uses the scientific method and the quality control methods typical of science: peer review. Studies of eyewitness identification include laboratory studies, field studies of simulated eyewitness events and of actual criminal investigations, and archival studies of actual criminal investigations. Most studies are conducted in laboratories because it is only in laboratories that we can know whether witnesses have made accurate or mistaken identifications given that the identity of the perpetrator is known in laboratory studies and usually unknown (or uncertain at best) in field studies. It is instructive to first consider laboratory research methods, as they are typically the most controlled studies, which allow for causal conclusions to be drawn about which factors contribute to increased rates of mistaken identifications. After considering the results of laboratory studies, we will move to the findings from field studies and archival studies of actual criminal investigations.

Laboratory Experiments

In most laboratory studies, university undergraduate students serve as eyewitnesses to simulated crimes. Sometimes, but not often, researchers use a sample of nonuniversity students as participants. The witnesses view a simulated crime enactment, such as an innocuous staged event in a classroom or laboratory or a videotaped simulation of a crime. Sometime later the witnesses are shown a photoarray and asked to identify the crime perpetrator. Studies typically rely on large sample sizes, usually dozens or hundreds of witnesses to the simulated crime.

Simulated crime studies have several common features. The goal of the stimulated crime study is to examine the impact of one or more specific factors on identification accuracy. Thus, one set of factors is held constant, while the researcher systematically manipulates one or more characteristics of the witnessing conditions or identification task. An investigator with interests in examining the effect of the passage of time between a crime and a photoarray on the accuracy of eyewitness identifications, for example, might expose a large sample of witnesses to the same simulated crime. The opportunity to view the perpetrator and the features of the photoarray test should be the same for each witness. The investigator would systematically manipulate the time delay between the crime and the identification. One group of eyewitnesses might view the photoarray after 1 week, and the other group might view the photoarray after 1 month. After all the data are collected, the investigator can use commonly accepted statistical techniques to determine whether identification accuracy rates vary systematically as a function of the time delay. By holding all conditions constant but systematically manipulating time delay, the investigator can test whether causal relations exist between time delay and identification accuracy.

INFO

Three common features of laboratory studies are

- systematic manipulation of independent variables
- random assignment
- perpetrator-absent and perpetrator-present lineups

SYSTEMATIC MANIPULATION OF INDEPENDENT VARIABLES

The *systematic manipulation of variables* is important for ruling out alternative explanations for research findings (Shadish, Cook, & Campbell, 2002). If variables are not manipulated independently of one another then it is impossible to determine which variable (or combination of variables) produced an effect on the outcome measure. An example of the interpretational problems that can arise from confounding the manipulation of two or more variables comes from a field study conducted in Illinois (Mecklenburg, 2006), which tested the effects of simultaneous versus sequential lineup presentation and double-blind versus single-blind lineup administration on the rates of suspect and foil identifications. The stated purpose of the field study was to examine differences in suspect and foil identification rates obtained using current procedures for conducting lineups (simultaneous presentation, single-blind administration) as opposed to recommended procedures (sequential presentation, double-blind administration in which the lineup administrator does not know the identity of the suspect). This study found that simultaneous single-blind lineup administrations produced more identifications of the suspect and fewer identifications of known innocent foils than did sequential double-blind lineup administrations.

What is to be made of these findings? Because all sequential lineups were administered by an officer who was blind to the suspect's identity and all simultaneous lineups were administered by an officer who knew which lineup member was the suspect, it is impossible to disentangle the effects of presentation type from the effects of administrator knowledge. Although the data from this study showed a decrease in suspect identifications with the new procedures, because of the confounding of presentation type and administrator knowledge we do not know whether this change was the result of adopting sequential presentation, double-blind administration, or both (not to mention it is unclear whether the reduction in suspect identifications represents a decrease in correct identifications, false identifications, or both because the identity of the true perpetrator is unknown).

RANDOM ASSIGNMENT

Random assignment is another common feature of laboratory studies. Researchers randomly assign witnesses to the experimental conditions. In the above example, the assignment of witnesses to time delay conditions should be randomly determined. The purpose of random assignment is to attempt to randomly distribute individual differences or any other preexisting differences among participants across conditions; random assignment allows one to conclude that any differences between groups is because of the manipulated factor that differs between groups and not any preexisting differences in members assigned to the groups.

Despite the confound in its design, the Illinois field study on eyewitness identification procedures did include random assignment as a feature in its design. Witnesses were randomly assigned to view a simultaneous single-blind lineup or a sequential double-blind lineup. Random assignment to condition allows us to rule out a variety of alternative explanations for the findings that simultaneous single-blind lineups produce more suspect identifications than do sequential double-blind lineups, including differences in the length of time the witness viewed the perpetrator, the level of stress the witnessed experienced while witnessing the event, lighting conditions, and witness age, to name but a few. Random assignment allows the research to presume that characteristics of the witness and the witnessed event are equivalent across the two lineup administration conditions.

PERPETRATOR-ABSENT AND PERPETRATOR-PRESENT PHOTOARRAYS AND LINEUPS

A third common factor in eyewitness research is the use of perpetrator-present and perpetrator-absent photoarrays. In defining the terms associated with eyewitness identification accuracy in chapter 2, we distinguished between correct and false suspect identifications, filler identifications, and correct and incorrect rejections. To obtain these different indices of identification accuracy, perpetrator-present and -absent photoarrays are needed. Perpetrator-present photoarrays simulate situations in which the suspect is the perpetrator and enable the investigator to assess the impact of the factor of interest (e.g., time delay in the example above) on rates of correct suspect identifications, filler identifications, and incorrect rejections. Perpetrator-absent photoarrays, by contrast, simulate situations in which the suspect is not the perpetrator (i.e., the suspect is innocent) and enable the investigator to assess the impact of the factor of interest on rates of false suspect identifications, filler identifications, and correct rejections. Assignment to condition (perpetrator-present or -absent) is random. Typically, the same fillers are used for perpetrator-present and -absent photoarrays, but the perpetrator is replaced with a similar-looking suspect in the perpetrator-absent photoarray.

BENEFITS AND LIMITATIONS

The laboratory research methodology has both benefits and limitations. The benefits include the high degree of experimental control, that is, the ability to hold many factors constant while systematically manipulating one or more variables. This level of control is critical for testing causal relations between general impairment factors and identification accuracy and between suspect bias factors and identification accuracy. The use of university students as participants is also an advantage. University students are intelligent, cooperative, and motivated to perform well. Another important benefit of laboratory research is the investigator's ability to designate individuals as the perpetrator, fillers, and innocent suspects. The designation of individuals for these roles ensures that the investigator can determine with certainty the accuracy or inaccuracy of the witnesses' identification decisions.

The laboratory research methodology also has limitations. The crime is simulated, and as such, the experience of the witness may differ in qualitative ways from the experiences of witnesses to actual crimes. The identifications, whether accurate or inaccurate, have no real consequences for the persons identified (or not identified). Nor does an identification decision in the laboratory have consequences for society as a whole. In actual cases, when a witness fails to identify the real perpetrator from a lineup or mistakenly identifies the wrong person, the real culprit remains free and may commit additional crimes. University students may be desirable as witnesses for the qualities mentioned above (e.g., intelligent, cooperative, motivated to perform well), but laboratory research is sometimes criticized because university students do not resemble the population of crime witnesses. Based on these limitations, critics (e.g., Mecklenburg, 2006) argue that, because crime simulations fail to replicate the conditions under which people witness actual crimes, there is no guarantee that the results from crime simulation research will generalize to what occurs in actual crimes.

These concerns about the external validity of laboratory research on eyewitness memory, however, are not universally shared. Many experts believe that the laboratory research does generalize and believe that the eyewitness research on many factors is sufficiently conclusive to warrant expert testimony (Kassin et al., 2001). Further, a growing number of police departments have adopted reforms in their identification procedures based on laboratory research (Wells, 2006), and by doing so have expressed confidence in the external validity of the research.

Field Research

In recognition of some of the oft-cited limitations associated with laboratory research methods, some investigators have conducted *field studies*. Field studies are crime simulation studies that are conducted in the community using ordinary citizens rather than in laboratories with university students as participants. Field studies have been conducted in convenience stores (e.g., Brigham, Maass, Snyder, & Spaulding, 1982; Krafka & Penrod, 1985; Platz & Hosch, 1988) and in banks (Pigott, Brigham, & Bothwell, 1990). Field studies can have some of the main benefits of laboratory studies, including good control over conditions, the ability to manipulate factors of interest, random assignment, and the ability to assess the accuracy of identifications with certainty. Field studies more closely represent the conditions under which witnesses sometimes view perpetrators. Field studies do not simulate dangerous crimes but rather expose citizens to suspicious individuals.

Crime Studies

A small but growing number of studies examine eyewitness identifications in actual crimes. Some of these studies are *archival* (e.g., Behrman & Davey, 2001; Behrman & Richards, 2005; Tollestrup, Turtle, & Yuille, 1994; Wright & McDaid, 1996), whereas others are *prospective* studies using actual crimes (e.g., Klobuchar, Steblay, & Caligiuri, 2006; Mecklenburg, 2006; Valentine, Pickering, & Darling, 2003; Wright & Skagerberg, 2007). Some of these studies attempt to isolate the impact of specific factors on identification performance. For example, the Illinois Pilot Study (Mecklenburg, 2006) compared eyewitness identification performance among actual crime witnesses shown sequentially-presented double-blind lineups versus nonblind simultaneously presented lineups. Studies of actual crimes, both archival and prospective studies, have the advantage of high degrees of realism because they are based on actual witnesses, crimes, and investigations.

Although high in realism, crime studies have other serious limitations. First, some studies attempt to examine the influence of crime violence on identification accuracy but have no direct measure of crime violence (e.g., Behrman & Davey, 2001; Tollestrup et al., 1994). Instead, they classify witnesses as bystanders and victims (and as victims of robbery vs. fraud in Tollestrup et al., 1994) and examine the influence of this proxy variable on identification accuracy. The proxy variable has limitations as a measure of crime violence, as acknowledged in both studies. These studies find different patterns of results for crime violence, and error associated with the measurement of crime violence may account for the disparate results.

Another limitation is that in some studies (e.g., Behrman & Davey, 2001; Mecklenburg, 2006; Tollestrup et al., 1994) the variables of interest are not independently manipulated and/or participants are not randomly assigned to conditions. Given these methods, some variables may be confounded with one another. For example, in Tollestrup et al. (1994), the authors acknowledge their measure of crime violence (bystander vs. victims) may be confounded with both exposure time to the perpetrator and time between the crime and the identification. In addition to the potential for confounds between independent variables, any relations between variables are correlational and therefore may be the product of third (unmeasured) variables. In archival research, it is very difficult to establish causal relations between variables because it is difficult to rule out alternative explanations for the relation between two variables.

Another main limitation associated with studies of actual crimes is that we typically do not know with certainty whether the suspect identifications are accurate or inaccurate. It is of limited helpfulness to know that some factor associated with a crime or manner in which a photoarray is conducted increases the likelihood of suspect identifications if we do not know whether the suspects identified are actually guilty or innocent. Some researchers (e.g., Behrman & Davey, 2001) attempted to identify cases for which there is additional and diagnostic evidence against the suspect besides the identification and analyzed those cases separately. Although such efforts may increase our confidence in the guilt of the suspect in some cases, they are still imperfect measures, and there is still considerable uncertainty about the accuracy of the suspect identifications in the many cases in which extrinsic evidence is of minimal probative value or is nonexistent (see Behrman & Davey, 2001). In recognition of this serious limitation, some studies (e.g., Behrman & Davey, 2001; Mecklenburg, 2006) have used filler identifications as a measure of known errors, as filler identifications are the only identifications that are known for certain to be incorrect. Using this logic, a factor that produces more filler identifications can be thought of as undesirable; a factor that decreases filler identifications can be seen as reducing known errors.

This logic, however, is problematic when we lack information about the quality of the fillers and about why witnesses are choosing fillers (Wells, 2008). Consider the following example. In one lineup procedure (Condition A), the investigator does not know which lineup member is the suspect and therefore cannot influence the eyewitness to identify the suspect. In another lineup procedure (Condition B), the investigator does know the suspect's identity and subtly conveys this information to the witness so that the witness knows with some degree of certainty which lineup member is the suspect. The witness in Condition B will be less likely to identify a filler than the witness in Condition A, but we certainly would not conclude that Condition B is a better procedure than Condition A just because it produces fewer filler identifications.

Yet another potential problem with filler identifications is that sometimes filler identifications are counted as nonidentifications (Behrman & Davey, 2001; Mecklenberg, 2006; Wells, 2008). How does this happen? Imagine a situation in which a witness identifies a lineup member but expresses uncertainty about the accuracy of his choice (e.g., "Number 3 looks like her" or "It might be Number 3 but I am not sure"). It is possible that lineup administrators may record different information depending upon whether they are blind to the suspect's identity. If the administrator knows that the suspect is Number 3, then this uncertain identification is likely to be recorded as a positive identification. If the administrator knows that Number 3 is a filler, it is possible that the administrator may record this uncertain identification as a nonidentification to avoid "burning" a witness, as witness who made a filler identification would likely be unusable at a later trial even if they eventually made a positive identification of a different suspect. In contrast, if the administrator does not know the identity of the suspect, then uncertain identifications cannot be differentially recorded based on whether the person identified is the suspect or a filler. If these processes are in play, the number of filler identifications reported in archival studies of nonblind lineup administrations may be an underestimate of the number of actual filler identifications. Further, when filler identifications are sometimes coded as lineup rejections, the analyses of the effects of specific factors on filler identifications become suspect. In sum, studies of actual crimes, like laboratory and field studies, have both benefits and drawbacks.

3
chapter

Meta-analysis

The development of a large and diverse literature on eyewitness identification has made meta-analytic techniques attractive and influential. *Meta-analysis* is a methodology for reviewing sets of studies to reach general conclusions about specific phenomena, examining trends across studies, and identifying variables that qualify the effects of certain factors on identification accuracy. For example, Meissner and Brigham (2001) conducted a meta-analysis of the many studies of the reliability of identifications made of own- versus other-race perpetrators. Their objectives included making general statements about the relative accuracy of own- and other-race identifications and examining whether this difference was qualified by other factors, such as the specific races of the witnesses and to-be-recognized targets and the amount of experience witnesses had with members of the other races. Meta-analysis can be thought of as averaging the results across studies, with studies differentially weighted based on the number of participants in them (i.e., studies with more participants are given proportionately greater weight when determining the average effect than those with fewer participants). When a large set of studies with varying methodologies and from a variety of labs converge on a conclusion through meta-analysis, we can be more confident in the meta-analytic conclusions. Meta-analyses are cited frequently in scholarly literature and in court.

Summary of Research Methodology

Each methodology contributes uniquely to our understanding of eyewitness identification and the psychological processes influencing it. Each method also has limitations. At present, however, the number of field studies of eyewitness identification is very small, and the number that has been published in refereed sources is smaller still (Behrman & Davey, 2001; Behrman & Richards, 2005; Valentine et al., 2003; Wright & McDaid, 1996; Wright & Skagerberg, 2007). Further, results of field studies are occasionally inconsistent, as noted below. Opponents of lab studies or of expert testimony may wish to point to the results of one or more field studies that seemingly contradict the conclusions of laboratory research as a means of attempting to discredit laboratory research. It behooves the expert, therefore, to be well-versed in the limitations of field studies so that such attempts can be effectively exposed as lacking in intellectual merit.

Having reviewed the basic methodology of eyewitness research, we now turn to our review of the common conclusions in research on eyewitness identifications. These conclusions are often the subject of expert testimony. Consistent with the discussion of key terms in chapter 2, we summarize research on general impairment factors, suspect bias factors, postdictors of identification accuracy, and admissibility issues. For each factor reviewed, we provide summaries of one or two relevant experiments to give the reader an idea about how scientific research is

BEST PRACTICE

Be familiar with the benefits and limitations of the different research methodologies, including

- laboratory research
- field studies
- studies of actual crimes
- meta-analysis

conducted. We then summarize the results of meta-analyses of comprehensive reviews where meta-analytic results are available. These results contain general statements about individual factors across sets of studies (in some cases across large numbers of studies). Last, some of the factors have been examined in studies of actual crimes. The results of these studies are of interest because they come from actual crimes, but the limitations—as summarized above in the research methods section and as acknowledged by the authors—must be given careful consideration.

3
chapter

General Impairment Factors

Own-Race Bias

The various factors in eyewitness testimony are illustrated in Figure 3.1. Although witnesses of one race are generally no more accurate at identifying perpetrators than are witnesses of other races, and perpetrators of one race are no more easily recognized than perpetrators of another race, witnesses are more accurate at recognizing same-race perpetrators than other-race perpetrators. Conversely, witnesses make more mistakes when attempting to identify other-race perpetrators than same-race perpetrators. This *own-race bias* appears to generalize across races.

Platz and Hosch (1988) conducted a field study in which White, Black, or Hispanic customers visited convenience clerks at stores

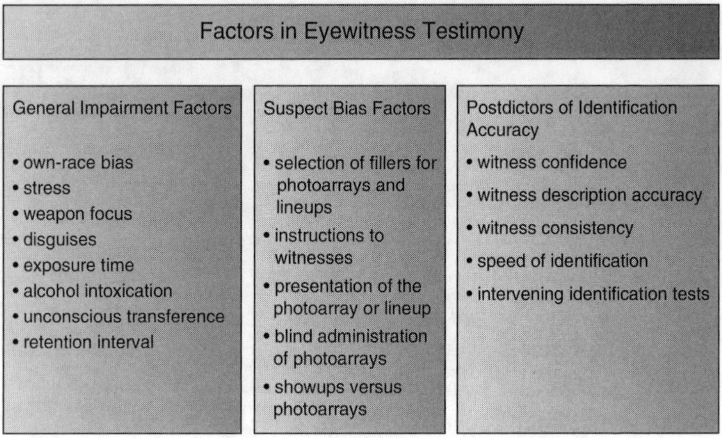

Figure 3.1 Factors in eyewitness testimony.

throughout El Paso, Texas, and had interactions with 90 White, Black, or Hispanic clerks. The customers engaged in behaviors that would make them salient to the clerks (e.g., paying for their purchase entirely with pennies). Two to three hours after each visit, an investigator asked the clerk to identify the customer from customer-present photoarrays constructed by a detective in the El Paso Police Department. White clerks were more likely to correctly recognize White customers (53%) than Black (40%) or Hispanic (34%) customers. Black clerks were more likely to correctly recognize Black (64%) than White (55%) or Hispanic (45%) customers. Hispanic clerks were more likely to correctly recognize Hispanic (54%) than White (36%) or Black (25%) customers. In an effort to examine the cross-race effect with Asian witnesses, Ng and Lindsay (1994) had 120 Asian and White participants study pictures of 24 Asian and White people and then gave them a recognition test consisting of the faces they had studied and some new faces. Asian participants were more accurate at recognizing Asian faces than White faces, and White subjects were more accurate at recognizing White faces than Asian faces. They replicated their study with another sample of 14 White and 91 Asian subjects. A study of identifications from actual crimes (Behrman & Davey, 2001) found that suspects were less likely to be identified in cross-race cases than in same-race cases, but another field study found that suspect identifications did not differ as a function of same- versus cross-race cases (Valentine et al., 2003).

One explanation for the own-race bias in witness identification accuracy centers on the degree of contact that people have with other races. Is it possible that the own-race bias exists because many people have limited contact with people of other races? If so, is it also possible that those who have

INFO

Studies support the existence of own-race bias, that is, witnesses are more accurate at identifying same-race perpetrators than other-race perpetrators. Likewise, they make more mistakes when attempting to identify other-race perpetrators than same-race perpetrators.

extensive contact with those of other races may be less prone to exhibiting this bias? This possibility has been investigated using two primary methods: testing groups of people who differ in degree of interracial contact and measuring individuals' levels of interracial contact through self-report. An example of the group difference method comes from a study of own-race bias among basketball fans and those who do not follow basketball (Li, Dunning, & Malpass, 1998). Because most basketball players are Black and fans would have experience attempting to identify particular players (requiring them to differentiate one player from another), it was anticipated that White fans would be better at identifying Black faces than would White nonfans. Other studies that have examined group differences in own-race bias based on whether group members live in integrated neighborhoods have failed to find that contact consistently reduces the own-race bias, with some studies finding group differences and others not (for a review of this literature, see Meissner & Brigham, 2001).

A meta-analysis of 31 studies reporting 91 tests of the accuracy of own- versus other-race identifications involving over 5,000 participants supports the finding of an own-race bias in eyewitness reliability (Meissner & Brigham, 2001). With respect to false identifications, White participants exhibited a larger own-race bias than did Black participants; the size of the own-race bias was comparable for White and Black participants with respect to correct identifications. Brief exposure times exacerbated the own-race bias as did longer retention intervals. The meta-analysis revealed no evidence of a relation between racial prejudice and the size of witnesses' own-race bias.

Stress

Some witnesses, such as those who are victims of armed robbery, encounter crime perpetrators under very stressful circumstances. Others, in contrast, encounter perpetrators under less stressful situations, such as spotting a suspicious-looking individual before or after a crime is committed when there is no apparent threat of danger to or victimization of the eyewitness. The relation between stress and accuracy is thought to follow an inverted-U-shaped relation. Moderate levels of stress are thought to improve orienting responses and cognitive processing, increasing attention to informative details of an event, but very high levels of stress are thought to interfere with cognitive processing. Consequently, we would expect moderate levels of stress to improve identification accuracy and very high levels of stress to lead to reductions in accuracy (Deffenbacher, 1980).

In an early study of the effects of stress, Clifford and Scott (1978) showed 48 college students either violent or nonviolent videotaped scenes in which two policemen are searching for a criminal and attempting to get help in their search from a third person who is reluctant to provide that help. In the violent film, the third person's reluctance to assist the police leads to a violent altercation, including thrown punches, and the officers physically restrain the person; in the nonviolent version, the third person's reluctance leads only to a verbal disagreement among the parties and feeble attempts at restraining the third party by one of the two police officers. After participants watched one of the two videos, they were tested for their recall of the events' details. Those that viewed the violent event were less accurate in their recall.

In a more recent and more ecologically valid study, Morgan et al. (2004) investigated the impact of extreme versus mild stress on identification accuracy in a sample of 530 active-duty military personnel enrolled in military survival school training. As part of their training, some participants experienced two types of interrogation: a high-stress interrogation with real physical confrontation and a low-stress interrogation without physical confrontation. Other participants experienced either high- or low-stress interroga-

INFO

Studies show that high-stress conditions experienced by the witness may impair witness memory.

tions. Participants—as eyewitnesses to the interrogation—attempted to identify their interrogators from lineups that were either live (simultaneous presentation) or photographic (simultaneous or sequential presentation). Among eyewitnesses shown interrogator-present, live lineups, the percent of correct identifications was much higher in the low-stress condition (62%) than in the high-stress condition (27%). False identification rates from interrogator-absent, live lineups were not affected by stress conditions. The same pattern held for simultaneously presented perpetrator-present photographic lineups (76% vs. 36%) and sequentially presented perpetrator-present photographic lineups (75% vs. 49%, respectively), and again, stress did not significantly influence identification performance in the corresponding perpetrator-absent lineup conditions.

Several studies of actual crimes attempted to examine the influence of stress by comparing suspect identification rates for victims of either more violent or less violent crimes. For example, Tollestrup and colleagues (1994) compared robbery victims, robbery witnesses, and fraud victims. The results from these archival studies do not present a clear pattern of relations between victimization type and suspect identification rates (Behrman & Davey, 2001; Tollestrup et al., 1994; Valentine et al., 2003). Moreover, witness and crime type have limitations as measures of witness stress, as noted above.

A meta-analysis by Deffenbacher, Bornstein, Penrod, and McGorty (2004) examined the effect of stress in 27 separate tests involving over 1,700 participant-witnesses. The studies included in the meta-analysis were limited to studies that include an experimental manipulation that produced a difference in experienced stress, excluding those studies for which manipulations did not produce either a change in the physiological state of witnesses or a change in witnesses' self-reported arousal. The results clearly showed that stress had a negative impact on identification accuracy. The authors concluded that high stress reduced the likelihood of correct identification but did not significantly influence the likelihood of false identification. The negative effects of stress on witness accuracy were stronger in studies that more faithfully recreated an eyewitness situation as opposed to a facial recognition paradigm in which participants were shown many faces and then had to distinguish new from old faces for the identification task. Stress similarly affected the identification of both children and adults.

Weapon Focus

The visual presence of a weapon tends to draw the attention of the witness. Our capacity for attention is limited. When a weapon is present and we turn our attention toward it, we have less attention to deploy toward a perpetrator's physical and facial characteristics. Consequently, when a weapon is visually present, we less effectively encode the perpetrator's characteristics and are less likely to accurately identify the perpetrator as compared to when there is no weapon visually present. Known as the *weapon focus effect*, this phenomenon has received considerable support in the research literature.

In one study (O'Rourke, Cutler, Penrod, & Stuve, 1989), 120 community members viewed a videotaped crime enactment. In half of the videotapes a weapon was present, and in half the weapon was absent. Seven days later, each eyewitness was shown either a perpetrator-present or a perpetrator-absent videotaped lineup. The weapon-hidden group showed a correct identification rate of 55%, whereas the weapon-present group showed a correct identification rate of 37%—a statistically significant difference. Steblay (1992) conducted a meta-analysis of six studies reporting 19 separate tests of the weapon focus effect with over 2,000 witnesses. The weapon focus effect was small but statistically significant, and the effect was larger in studies that better approximated crime situations (higher levels of stress for the witness). Studies of actual crimes reveal mixed effects of the influence of weapon presence on suspect identifications (Behrman & Davey, 2001; Tollestrup et al., 1994; Valentine et al., 2003).

What psychological processes are responsible for the weapon focus effect? One possibility is that a weapon draws attentional focus away from other features of a witnessed event. Loftus, Loftus, and Messo (1987) employed a corneal reflection device, allowing researchers to track eye movements of subjects, noting both number and duration of eye fixations. Their study provided direct evidence that eye fixation on a weapon is a critical correlate of reduced identification accuracy. It does not appear, however, that a weapon is necessary to cause this reallocation of attention away from a perpetrator's face. Pickel (1999) independently varied the threat and the unusualness of an object carried by a perpetrator in a videotaped crime reenactment set in a hair salon. The high-threat items were scissors (usual) and a gun (unusual); the low-threat items were a raw chicken (unusual) and a wallet (usual). Although the type of object did not affect identification accuracy, participants did remember fewer details about the perpetrator when she held an unusual object rather than a typical object for the setting; the potential threat of the object did not affect memory for details.

Disguises

It is obvious that the wearing of a disguise that masks a perpetrator's facial and physical characteristics can impair identification accuracy, yet more subtle disguises can also impair identification accuracy. Cutler, Penrod, and Martens (1987a), for example, showed 165 college students a videotaped crime enactment. In half of the videotapes the perpetrator wore a cap that covered his hair and hairline, and in the other half, the perpetrator wore no hat. All witnesses later attempted to identify the perpetrator from a lineup. Of the witnesses who viewed the perpetrator without the cap, 45% made correct decisions on the lineup test as compared to 27% of the witnesses who viewed the perpetrator whose hair and hairline were covered.

Cutler and colleagues tested for the effects of a disguise on eyewitness reliability in several additional studies. Cutler (2006) reviewed the set of six studies (over 1,300 witnesses) that examined identification accuracy for perpetrators who wore a cap covering their hair and hairlines as compared to the same perpetrators with their heads uncovered. Identification accuracy was significantly reduced when the perpetrators' hats were uncovered. Other research shows that changes in glasses, hairstyle, and facial hair and age-related changes can also impair identification accuracy (Read, 1995; Read, Tollestrup, Hammersley, McFadzen, & Christensen, 1990).

Exposure Time

Exposure time refers to the amount of time that the witness is able to view the perpetrator's facial and physical characteristics. With more time, witnesses are able to more effectively encode the perpetrator's physical and facial characteristics, thus facilitating identification accuracy. For example, in a study by Laughery, Alexander, and Lane (1971), 128 subjects were shown 150 slides of peoples' faces. Each face was shown for 10 or 32 s. Participants then viewed another set of 150 faces, some of which they had seen before and some that they had not seen before. Subjects were better able to recognize faces that they had seen for 32 s than for 10 s.

In a more recent study (Memon, Hope, & Bull, 2003), 64 young adults (ages 17–25) and older adults (ages 59–81) watched a videotaped reconstruction of a robbery in which the perpetrator's face could be seen for either 12 or 45 s. Each witness then attempted to identify the robber from a perpetrator-present or perpetrator-absent photoarray. Exposure duration had a significant impact on identification accuracy. Ninety-five percent of the young adults and 85% of the older adults made correct identifications from the perpetrator-present photoarrays when the robber was exposed for 45 s, but only 29% of the young adults and 35% of the older adults made correct identifications when the robber was exposed for 12 s. Similarly, 41% of the younger adults and 50% of the older adults made false identifications from the perpetrator-absent photoarrays when the target was exposed for 45 s, but 90% of the younger adults and 80% of the older adults made false identifications when the robber was exposed for only 12 s.

INFO

Longer exposures to the perpetrator are associated with more correct identifications by witnesses.

In their meta-analysis of face recognition and eyewitness identification research, Shapiro and Penrod (1986) demonstrated the reliability of exposure time effects on eyewitness accuracy. They reviewed eight tests of the effects of increased exposure time on correct identifications with almost 1,000 participants. Exposure time had a moderate to large effect on the rates of correct identifications $(d = .61)$ with longer exposure times leading to more correct identifications (or hits). They also reviewed eight tests of the effects of exposure time on rates of false alarms (or mistaken identifications) with 1,389 participants. Although the effect size was smaller $(d = .22)$ for mistaken identifications, shorter exposure times remained related to more witness mistakes. In a study of actual crimes (Klobuchar et al., 2006; Valentine et al., 2003), suspects were more likely to be identified following longer rather than shorter exposure times but exposure time was unrelated to the mistaken identification of a foil (Valentine et al., 2003).

Alcohol Intoxication

Occasionally, crimes take place in environments in which alcohol consumption occurs and one or more witnesses are under the influence of alcohol at the time of the crime. Considerable psychological research has demonstrated that alcohol intoxication impairs cognitive functioning and performance on a wide variety of tasks. The negative effects of alcohol intoxication on memory have been found to generalize to eyewitness identifications from showups and photoarrays (Dysart, 2008).

In a field study, Dysart, Lindsay, MacDonald, and Wicke (2002) examined the impact of alcohol intoxication on showup identifications. Two women investigators approached patrons of a bar and invited them to participate in their study. Patrons who agreed were led to another room and left with a male experimenter to complete the first phase of the experiment. Each patron participated in a filler task, had her intoxication level assessed with a breathalyzer, and attempted to identify the woman who recruited her from a photograph. Half of the participants were shown the recruiter's photo (resembling the guilty suspect scenario), and the other half were shown a look-alike (resembling the innocent suspect scenario). Blood alcohol level was significantly associated with the tendency to commit false identifications but was not significantly associated with the tendency to make correct identifications. When participants were divided into groups by blood alcohol level, the rate of false identifications was 22% for those in the low-intoxication group (BAL of .02% on average) but 52% for the high-intoxication group (BAL of .09% on average). The corresponding correct identification rates were 68% and 62%, respectively.

In a laboratory study of the effect of alcohol intoxication on eyewitness memory, Read, Yuille, and Tollestrup (1992) found that alcohol intoxication was associated with lower identification accuracy rates from lineups for witnesses in a low arousal condition. In a high arousal condition, intoxication was not significantly associated with identification accuracy. Intoxication level did not influence false identification rates in the Read et al. study. Although the number of studies examining the effects of intoxication on identification accuracy is small (these are the only two we could find) and the results are mixed, the much larger body of research showing that alcohol impairs cognitive processing in general (Steele & Josephs, 1990)

INFO

Alcohol intoxication at the time of the crime may negatively impact the accuracy of eyewitness identifications.

leads us to conclude that alcohol intoxication is a general impairment factor that decreases the accuracy of eyewitness identifications.

Unconscious Transference

Sometimes witnesses mistakenly identify as a crime perpetrator a person who is familiar to them but was not the perpetrator of the crime; we refer to this type of error as *unconscious transference*. It is thought to be an "unconscious" error because the witness does not recall that the person is familiar because of exposure to that person from some context other than the witnessed crime. If witnesses are aware that they are familiar with the person from another context but nevertheless mistakenly identify the person as a crime perpetrator, this would be an example of conscious transference.

Several studies have examined unconscious transference. According to a recent review of this literature, some of these studies find that a familiar person is more likely to be mistakenly identified than an unfamiliar person, whereas other studies find that familiarity does not influence the likelihood of mistaken identification (Ross, Marsil, & Metzger, 2008). Ross et al. report that "reverse transference" has occurred in research; sometimes familiar persons are less likely to be mistakenly identified than unfamiliar persons.

Read et al. (1990) conducted five experiments, each of which involved a perpetrator-absent lineup. These were field experiments involving the witnessing of bystanders and targets by retail store clerks or by students in university classrooms going about their normal routines. Only one study produced transference errors. In Read et al. (1990, Exp 5), an audio technician interrupted a class to fix the broken sound system. Prior to the interruption by the technician, transference witnesses were exposed to a bystander who was seen in a context outside the classroom (i.e., distributing exam material in another class, notifying a class that the instructor would be late). Control witnesses were exposed to the technician but not the bystander. Two weeks later, all witnesses were asked to identify the technician from a photo lineup that contained the bystander and four unfamiliar foils. Approximately twice as many of the transference witnesses misidentified the bystander as compared with the control subjects. Moreover, 23% of the transference witnesses who misidentified the bystander indicated they had seen him in a context other than at the scene of the crime (conscious transference).

Meta-analysis is a particularly useful method for synthesizing literatures that are characterized by mixed findings, as is the unconscious transference literature. Deffenbacher, Bornstein, and Penrod (2006) meta-analyzed 19 tests of the transference effect (i.e., the mistaken identification of someone seen previously as the perpetrator of a crime). Across these 19 tests, there was a significant effect of a transference condition (i.e., previous exposure to an innocent person) on the likelihood of transference errors (i.e., the mistaken identification of that innocent person as the perpetrator of a witnessed event). Deffenbacher and his colleagues also analyzed whether there were variables that moderated the size of the transference effect, including whether the previous viewing of the innocent target was in a bystander situation or through mugshot exposure. Although the transference effects were statistically reliable under both conditions, the transference effect is larger when the mistakenly identified person has previously been seen in a mugshot. Thus, the results for transference research are rather mixed but in their aggregate suggest small but reliable transference errors. Ross et al. (2008) argue that transference errors are more likely to occur when the familiar person and the perpetrator are moderately similar in appearance and when the witness consciously infers that the familiar person and the perpetrator are the same person.

Retention Interval

Retention interval refers to the amount of time that has passed between a crime and an eyewitness identification. In some crimes the identification takes place immediately after the crime in the form of on-the-scene showups. In other cases, the identification may take place weeks, months, or even years after the identification. The length of the retention interval is inversely related to identification accuracy.

Krafka and Penrod (1985), for example, conducted a field experiment in which 85 naïve convenience store clerks were asked to identify— from customer-present or -absent photoarrays—a previously encountered customer either 2 or 24 hr after the encounter. False identifica-

INFO

Identifications that take place soon after the crime are more likely to be correct, and identifications that take place long after the crime are more likely to be mistaken.

tions from customer-absent photoarrays were far more prevalent after 24 hr (52%) than after 2 hr (15%). When the customer was present in the photoarrays, the difference in retention interval did not affect performance (43% vs. 39%, respectively). Cutler, Penrod, O'Rourke, and Martens (1986) showed 287 undergraduate students videotaped crime enactment and attempted identifications from photographic lineups after either 7 or 28 days. The corresponding accuracy rates were 71% and 55%, respectively.

Shapiro and Penrod's (1986) aforementioned meta-analysis supports the conclusion that retention interval is inversely associated with identification accuracy. Eighteen tests—with almost 2,000 participants—of the effects of retention interval on the rate of correct identifications (hits) revealed that retention interval had a moderate effect on accuracy ($d = .43$), with longer retention intervals resulting in fewer correct identifications. Fourteen tests (1,868 participants) of the effects of retention interval on mistaken identifications (false alarms) revealed a somewhat smaller but still significant effect ($d = .33$), with longer retention intervals increasing mistaken identifications. In studies of actual crimes, witnesses identified fewer suspects as time between the crime and the identification test increased (Behrman & Davey, 2001; Tollestrup et al., 1994), but this effect is not universally obtained in archival studies (see Valentine et al., 2003).

Suspect Bias Factors
Selection of Fillers for Photoarrays and Lineups

Photoarray composition refers to the method of selecting fillers for the photoarray. Generally, there are two recognized approaches for selecting fillers. One method, labeled as *suspect-*

matched (SM) fillers, is to select fillers based on their resemblance to the suspect. The other method, labeled *perpetrator-description-matched* (PDM), involves selecting fillers that match the witness's description of the perpetrator. The difference between these two procedures is best understood in the context of suspect bias factors. Recall from chapter 2 that one of the reasons for which a witness might positively identify a suspect is that the witness is motivated to make a positive identification and is able to deduce which photo in the array is the suspect's. If the witness remembers the perpetrator's description and the suspect is the only person (or one of a very few persons) who matches that description of the perpetrator, the witness should be able identify the suspect from deduction rather than from memory. PDM photoarrays protect against this form of deduction because all persons in the photoarray match the perpetrator's description by design. The persons selected for SM photoarrays may but need not match the perpetrator's description. For this reason, PDM photoarrays are preferred over SM photoarrays.

Research comparing the two procedures shows that PDM photoarrays provide a better balance of increased correct identifications and decreased false identifications relative to SM photoarrays. Clark and Tunnicliff (2001), for example, staged a crime before 187 undergraduates and, 30 min later, showed witnesses photoarrays. Each witness was shown one of three types of photoarrays: (a) a perpetrator-present array in which the fillers were chosen based on their similarity to the perpetrator, (b) a perpetrator-absent array in which the fillers were matched to the innocent suspect, and (c) a perpetrator-absent array in which the fillers were matched to the perpetrator (e.g., the fillers used in the perpetrator-present array). Officers from the San Bernardino County Sheriff's Department selected fillers for the photoarrays in accordance with the experimental conditions. Witnesses who saw a perpetrator-absent array were significantly more likely to identify the innocent suspect from the SM photoarray than from the perpetrator-matched photoarray (25% vs. 5%). The authors called this the "backfire" effect: The selection of fillers based on their match to the innocent suspect produces a lineup in which the innocent suspect is the person most likely to be identified.

In another study of lineup composition effects, Wells, Rydell, and Seelau (1993) staged thefts before 252 undergraduates and constructed unique photospreads for each witness. Photospreads were either perpetrator-present or -absent. The fillers were selected to (a) resemble the suspect (SM), (b) match the witness's description of the culprit (PDM), or (c) not match the description of the perpetrator. When the perpetrator was present in the photoarray, witnesses who viewed the array in which the fillers did not match the perpetrator's description or PDM photoarrays were more likely to make correct identifications (about 70%) than were witnesses who viewed the SM photoarrays (about 20%). When the perpetrator was absent from the photoarray, false identifications were more prevalent among witnesses who viewed mismatch-description photoarrays (about 45%) than among witnesses who viewed SM or PDM photoarrays (about 10%). Thus, the photoarray that produced the best overall performance—more correct identifications and fewer false identifications—was the PDM photoarray.

INFO

The preferred method of choosing fillers is to match them to the witness's description of the perpetrator.

3
chapter

Instructions to Witnesses

Several of the suspect bias factors depend on the witnesses' motivation to make a positive identification. The instructions given to the witness prior to showing the photoarray can influence the witness's tendency to make a positive identification. Instructions that suggest that the perpetrator is present or suggest that the witness is expected to make a choice from the lineup (i.e., make a positive identification) increase the witness's inclination to positively identify someone (i.e., make a choice) from the photoarray. Conversely, instructions that convey the fact that the perpetrator's photo might not be in the array or otherwise emphasize that it is important to avoid the mistaken identification of an innocent suspect reduce the witness's inclination to identify someone from the photoarray.

This principle has been tested in several crime simulation studies. In the first published study of lineup instructions, Malpass and Devine (1981) staged an act of vandalism in view of 350 undergraduate students, 100 of whom were asked to identify the vandal from one of two live lineups (perpetrator-present or perpetrator-absent) within the next 3 days. Half received the following suggestive instruction: "We believe that the person is present in the lineup. Look carefully at each of the five individuals in the lineup. Which of these is the person you saw?" This form of instruction did not have a "none of the above" option. The other half received the following nonsuggestive instruction: "The person may be one of the five individuals in the lineup. It is also possible that she is not in the lineup. Look carefully at each of the five individuals in the lineup. If the person you saw is not in the lineup, circle 0. If the person is present in the lineup, circle the number of her position." Among witnesses who viewed the perpetrator-absent lineup, 78% who received suggestive instructions and 33% who received neutral instructions made false identifications. Among witnesses who viewed the perpetrator-present lineup, the accuracy rates were 75% and 83%, respectively.

In a study by Cutler, Penrod, and Martens (1987b), 290 undergraduate students viewed a videotaped crime enactment. Two or 14 days later, each eyewitness was shown either a perpetrator-present or a perpetrator-absent photoarray in which the instructions did or did not include an admonition stating that the perpetrator might not be in the lineup. Among witnesses shown perpetrator-absent lineups, false identifications were 87% for the suggestive instruction and 57% for the nonsuggestive instruction groups. Among witnesses shown perpetrator-present lineups, correct identifications were 61% for the suggestive instruction and 67% for the nonsuggestive instruction groups.

INFO

Biased instructions may increase the likelihood of false identification.

Steblay (1997) meta-analyzed 18 such studies reporting 19 separate tests and involving over 2,500 witnesses. She found that witnesses given biased instructions made significantly more false identifications from perpetrator-absent photoarrays than did witnesses given unbiased instructions. Among witnesses shown perpetrator-present photoarrays, instructions did not significantly influence identification performance. Clark (2005) has since published a qualitative reanalysis of the studies used in the meta-analysis. Based on this reanalysis, he argued that biased instructions produced a small increase in the likelihood of correct identification from perpetrator-present photoarrays. Both reviews agree that the reduction in mistaken identifications from perpetrator-absent arrays that comes from a warning that the perpetrator may not be in a lineup is larger than any reduction in correct identifications from perpetrator-present lineups that may also result from such a warning.

Presentation of the Photoarray or Lineup

Traditionally, most investigators present a set of photos or lineup members to the witness simultaneously and ask the witnesses to identify the perpetrator from among the set of photos (Wogalter, Malpass, & McQuiston, 2004). Researchers have compared this procedure with a procedure in which the presentation of photos or lineup members is done sequentially, wherein the witness is presented with each lineup member or photo individually and asked whether or not each person is the perpetrator. Crime simulation research has reliably shown that the sequential presentation of photoarrays, as compared to simultaneous presentation, significantly reduces the likelihood of false identification from perpetrator-absent photoarrays. Simultaneous presentation produces a small but reliable increase in correct identifications from perpetrator-present photoarrays; however, the reduction in false identifications achieved through sequential presentation is much larger than the increase in correct identifications associated with simultaneous presentation.

Lindsay and Wells (1985), in the first published study comparing simultaneous with sequential lineups, staged thefts before 243 undergraduates and in the same sessions had eyewitnesses attempt identifications from perpetrator-present or -absent photoarrays. Half of the witnesses saw simultaneous arrays and half saw

INFO

Sequential lineups are associated with a smaller likelihood of mistaken identification than simultaneous lineups.

sequential photoarrays. When the thief was present, the percent of correct identifications was comparable for simultaneous and sequential lineups (58% vs. 50%, respectively). When the thief was absent, simultaneous lineups produced more false identifications than did sequential lineups (43% vs. 17%). We consider simultaneous presentation to be a suspect bias factor because, like biased instructions, it increases the likelihood that a witness will make a choice from a lineup, particularly in perpetrator-present photoarrays.

Cutler and Penrod (1988) twice replicated this finding of the superiority of sequential lineups for reducing mistaken identifications. In their first study, 175 undergraduates watched a videotaped crime and attempted identifications 1 week later from videotaped lineups that were either simultaneous or sequential and target-present or -absent. When the thief was present, the percent of correct identifications was comparable for simultaneous and sequential lineups (76% vs. 80%, respectively). When the thief was absent, simultaneous lineups produced more false identifications than did sequential lineups (39% vs. 19%). The beneficial effect of sequential presentation was replicated in their second study.

Indeed, this pattern of results was confirmed by a meta-analysis by Steblay, Dysart, Fulero, and Lindsay (2001), in which they examined the results of 23 studies reporting 30 separate tests of simultaneous versus sequential presentation involving over 4,000 witnesses. Within perpetrator-present identification procedures, correct identifications were significantly more frequent in simultaneous as opposed to sequential lineups. In perpetrator-absent identification procedures, witnesses who viewed a sequential identification procedure were more likely to correctly reject the lineup and less likely to mistakenly identify a lineup member who was not the perpetrator than were witnesses who viewed a simultaneous identification procedure.

The benefits of sequential presentation have recently been challenged on the basis of the Illinois Pilot study (Mecklenburg, 2006), a prospective experiment involving several police departments. Briefly summarized, this study compared suspect identification rates following nonblind simultaneously presented lineups with sequentially presented double-blind lineups and found that suspect rates were higher and filler identifications lower in the former than in the latter. The results of this study have been used to support the contention that simultaneous presentation is superior to sequential presentation, but this conclusion is unjustified for several reasons. First, the study had no measure of the accuracy of the suspect identifications. Thus, given the likelihood that some percentage of the suspect identifications was incorrect, the results would likely show that nonblind simultaneous presentation produced more mistaken identifications than blind sequential presentations (as we would expect from the lab research). Second, the confounding of the presentation procedure with blind procedures makes it impossible to conclude that the results are due to simultaneous presentation (Schacter et al., 2008). Third, filler identifications are a poor measure of eyewitness performance in the absence of information about the resemblance between the fillers, perpetrator, and suspect and about the reasons for which witnesses are choosing the fillers, as articulated by Wells (2008). For these reasons, many commentators have concluded that the Illinois Pilot Study results do not inform the scientific community about the superiority of simultaneous or sequential procedures (Ross & Malpass, 2008; Schacter et al., 2008; Steblay, 2008; Wells, 2008).

Blind Administration of Photoarrays

The lead investigator in the case typically conducts the photoarray or lineup procedure. Because the lead investigator knows which photo is the suspect's, the investigator has the opportunity to advertently or inadvertently influence the witness to select a specific photo from the photoarray. Recall from chapter 2 that one of the alternative explanations for a positive identification (i.e., the witness making a choice from a photoarray) is influenced by the investigator. When the investigator knows which photo is the suspect's we call this *nonblind administration*, a suspect bias factor. Blind administration, by contrast, requires that the photoarray be conducted by an investigator who does not know which photo is the suspect's and therefore is unable to advertently or inadvertently steer the witness toward selecting the suspect's photo—rather than a filler's photo—from the array. The belief that an investigator can convey the suspect's identity to the witness through the use of subtle or overt cues is substantiated by a well-accepted literature on research methods examining how experimenters' expectations influence their participants' behaviors (see Rosenthal, 1976) and by several laboratory studies of eyewitness identification (Greathouse & Kovera, 2009; Haw & Fisher, 2004; Phillips, McAuliff, Kovera, & Cutler, 1999; Russano, Dickinson, Greathouse, & Kovera, 2006).

In the Phillips et al. (1999) study, 100 students were randomly assigned to role-play witnesses (50) and investigators (50). The 50 participants viewed a staged crime with two perpetrators (one male and one female) and were shown sequential or simultaneous perpetrator-absent photoarrays for each perpetrator by another participant who was blind to the suspect's identity for one of the arrays but not the other. Phillips et al. also manipulated the presence versus absence of an observer who was thought to be on the lookout for suggestive influence by the investigator (who was admonished to not clue the witness to the suspect's identity). When an observer was present and the photoarray was presented sequentially, false identifications were significantly more likely to occur with nonblind as opposed to blind procedures. This pattern was not present in the observer-absent or simultaneous presentation conditions.

Although other studies have identified other untoward effects of nonblind presentation (Garrioch & Brimacombe, 2001; Haw & Fisher, 2004), the effect is rather elusive in lab studies of eyewitness identification (Russano et al., 2006). As Russano et al. (2006) explain, the influence may be subtle, difficult to observe, and difficult to simulate realistically in lab studies. More recent research (Greathouse & Kovera, 2009) suggests that the effects of investigator knowledge may be larger under conditions that increase the likelihood that the witness will make a positive identification, such as biased instructions or simultaneous presentation. The variability in the influence of administrator knowledge on eyewitness decisions across studies suggests that there are previously unidentified variables that moderate the effects of

single-blind lineup administration on eyewitness accuracy. It is possible that factors that increase the likelihood that a witness will make a choice from a lineup, such as the presence of biased lineup instructions or simultaneous lineup presentation, may increase the biasing effects of nonblind lineup administration. For example, if an administrator fails to remind the witness that the perpetrator may not be in the lineup, unsure witnesses may be more likely to search the investigator's behavior for cues to the suspect's identity because they assume that the administrator knows which lineup member they should be picking.

To test the possibility that factors that increase witnesses' likelihood of choosing a lineup member also increase the influence of administrator knowledge of a suspect's identity, Greathouse and Kovera manipulated whether the administrator had knowledge of the suspect's identity, the type of lineup (simultaneous vs. sequential), the presence of the actual perpetrator in the lineup, and the type of lineup instructions (biased vs. unbiased). Witnesses then made an identification from either a target-present or a target-absent lineup.

When witnesses received biased instructions and simultaneous lineups, they were more likely to make suspect identifications in single-blind than in double-blind lineups (Greathouse & Kovera, 2009). The pattern of filler and suspect identifications suggests that the increase in mistaken identifications under single-blind conditions was the result of nonblind administrators influencing witnesses who would have, under double-blind conditions, made filler identifications to make suspect identifications instead. In essence, it appears that administrators who knew the identity of the suspect shifted unsure witnesses' guesses from filler identifications to suspect identifications. Lineup administrator knowledge did not influence the rates at which witnesses rejected the lineup. Perhaps most important the diagnosticity of the identifications (the ratio of correct identifications in target-present lineups to mistaken identifications of the suspect in target-absent lineups) made under double-blind conditions was greater than the diagnosticity under single-blind conditions—two times greater. Given the much broader literature on expectancy effects cited above and the research specifically testing the influence of single-blind lineup administration on eyewitness identification accuracy, there is good reason to be concerned about the influence of nonblind presentation on eyewitness identification accuracy.

Showups Versus Photoarrays

In a showup, the investigator presents a single suspect to the witness for identification. Showups normally take place when a suspect is apprehended very soon after a crime (usually near the crime scene or following a chase) and the witness is still available for the identification procedure. Occasionally, the photographic equivalent of a showup is conducted using a single photo of the suspect. Showups can be evaluated from two perspectives. The first perspective examines the relative effect of conducting a showup as compared to showing a witness a photoarray on identification performance. One can think of a showup as a sequential presentation of a single suspect. From this perspective one might predict that witnesses would make fewer false identifications from showups than from simultaneously presented photoarrays because sequential procedures produce fewer mistaken identifications.

Yarmey, Yarmey, and Yarmey (2006) compared identification performance from showups and lineups in two studies. In their first study, each of the 565 community members was approached in public places by one of two experimenters asking for directions or seeking assistance in finding lost jewelry. Each participant was asked to identify the target from a target-present or -absent photographic showup or lineup immediately or after 30 min, 2, or 24 hr. In addition, the photographed target was shown wearing the same or different clothing from the original interaction. When the target was present in the identification

INFO

Showups are high in suspect bias, as positive identifications may be a result of guessing, deduction, and investigative influence.

test, showups produced significantly more correct identifications than did lineups. Overall, showups produced more correct identifications (61%) than did lineups (39%) but also produced more false identifications than did lineups (44% and 19%, respectively). The difference in false identification was most pronounced after longer delays and when the innocent suspect had clothing similar to the perpetrator's.

Yarmey et al.'s findings were confirmed in a meta-analysis of field and laboratory research (Steblay, Dysart, Fulero, & Lindsay, 2003). Generally, witnesses made fewer identifications from showups than from lineups and photoarrays. Thus, showups led to more correct rejections as compared to photoarrays and lineups. The risk of false identification from showups was greatest when the innocent suspect looked like the perpetrator. This meta-analysis examined the results of 8 studies, 12 separate tests of showups, and more than 3,000 witnesses. Although showups may lead to fewer positive identifications than photoarrays, according to the meta-analysis, they pose a serious risk as a suspect bias factor. Recall from chapter 2 that positive identifications (i.e., choices in an identification procedure) may be the product of a witness's memory for the perpetrator, but positive identifications may also be the result of guessing, deduction, or investigator influence. The main problem with showups, therefore, is that it is impossible to rule out guessing, deduction, and investigative influence (the investigator always knows the suspect's identity in a showup) as explanations of positive identifications, thus creating more doubt about whether the identification is the product of the witness's memory.

3
chapter

INFO

The confidence expressed by the witness is frequently used to assess the accuracy of eyewitness identification. It is so common that it is specifically named as a factor in U.S. law that judges should consider when evaluating the suggestiveness of particular identification procedures (*Manson v. Braithwaite*, 1977) and in jury instructions regarding the factors to take into consideration when evaluating eyewitness identifications (*United States v. Telfaire*, 1978).

Postdictors of Identification Accuracy

Postdictors of confidence is a "catch-all" category of variables that do not neatly fall into the previous two categories but are otherwise sometimes used to assess the accuracy of eyewitness identification.

Witness Confidence

Eyewitness confidence is probably the second-most commonly studied variable in the eyewitness identification literature (the first being identification accuracy). It is very common in studies of eyewitness identification to assess witness confidence after the witness has made an identification decision and to then examine the correlation between confidence and accuracy. There have been several meta-analyses of the relation between confidence and accuracy, the most recent and comprehensive of which was authored by Sporer, Penrod, Read, and Cutler (1995). This meta-analysis examined the results of 30 tests of the relation between confidence and accuracy involving over 4,000 witnesses. The relation between confidence and accuracy was modest in size overall and was significantly larger for witnesses who made a positive identification than for witnesses who rejected the lineup. The relation was also qualified by viewing conditions. Consistent with Deffenbacher's (1980) "optimality hypothesis," more optimal viewing conditions were associated with higher correlations between confidence and accuracy.

In a study by Cutler et al. (1987a), for example, 165 undergraduate students viewed a videotaped crime enactment under various conditions and attempted identifications from lineups either the same day or 1 week later. The confidence–accuracy correlation was .20. In another study, O'Rourke, Penrod, Cutler, and Stuve (1989) showed a videotaped crime enactment to 120 community members (members of a church group, parents of a local Boy Scouts troop, undergraduate summer school students). Each mock witness attempted an identification after 1 week. The correlation between confidence and accuracy was .28. In the aforementioned field study of the own-race bias in eyewitness identifications conducted (Platz & Hosch, 1988), the correlation between confidence and accuracy was .23.

CONFIDENCE MALLEABILITY

It is important to note that confidence correlates modestly with accuracy only under certain circumstances: when confidence is measured immediately after the identification and before the witness is provided with any information that validates or invalidates his identification. Considerable research has now shown that information that validates or invalidates a witness's identification, such as being told that a co-witness identified the same or a different person or receiving positive verbal reinforcement by the investigator, inflates confidence and attenuates the confidence–accuracy relation. In an early demonstration of this phenomenon, Luus and Wells (1994) staged a theft 70 times before pairs of eyewitnesses (140 eyewitnesses in total) each of whom then made a photo lineup identification. After making an identification, each witness received one of nine types of information regarding the alleged identification decision of their co-witness. Witnesses who were told that their co-witness identified the same person whom they had identified showed an increase in the confidence they expressed to a subject posing as a police officer. Confidence deflation occurred among witnesses who thought their co-witness either identified another person or had stated that the thief was not in the lineup. The

INFO

Witness confidence can be influenced by various factors after an identification is made, and these factors will reduce the correlation between confidence and accuracy.

effects of initial co-witness information were not mitigated by subsequent changes to that information.

Bradfield, Wells, and Olson (2002) found that information learned after an identification not only influenced confidence estimates but led witnesses to reappraise the conditions under which they witnessed the event. Bradfield et al. exposed 245 undergraduates to a 3 min video and had them attempt identifications from six-person culprit-present or -absent videotaped lineups in the same experimental session. Witnesses were given suggestive lineup instructions to ensure that they would make identifications. After making identifications, half of the participants were told by the investigator, "Good, you identified the actual suspect." The other half was given no such information. Witnesses in both groups were equally inaccurate. The relation between confidence and accuracy was significantly lower ($r = .37$) among witnesses who heard the confirming feedback than among witnesses who did not hear the confirming feedback ($r = .57$). Witnesses who heard the confirming feedback, in comparison to those who did not, reported having had a better view of the culprit, paying more attention to the video, having a better basis for their identification, making their identification more easily, being more willing to testify, and having a clearer image of the culprit's face in their mind. Similar findings have been reported in a study of actual crimes (Wright & Skagerberg, 2007).

A recent meta-analysis of 20 tests of the confidence malleability effect with over 2,400 participants confirms the robustness of the effect of feedback on witness ratings of confidence as well as their ratings of the quality of the witnessing conditions (Douglass & Steblay, 2006). The size of postidentification feedback's effect on witness certainty was significant and substantial in magnitude ($d = 79$), with confirming feedback increasing witnesses' confidence in the accuracy of their identifications. Although the postidentification feedback had a somewhat smaller effect on witnesses' estimates of how good of a view they had and how much attention they paid to the perpetrator—criteria by which judges evaluate the likely accuracy of eyewitness identifications—the feedback effect was still moderate in size ($ds = .50$ and $.46$, respectively). When witnesses testify about their confidence on the witness stand, months or years after a crime and following considerable postidentification learning, there is good reason to question the relation between confidence and accuracy.

Witness Description Accuracy

It is commonly argued that a witness who gives an incorrect description of a perpetrator does not have a good memory of the perpetrator and is unlikely to make a correct identification of the perpetrator. Conversely, a witness who gives a strikingly accurate description of a perpetrator has a good memory and should be able to correctly recognize the perpetrator. A small body of research has examined the relation between description accuracy and recognition accuracy. Description accuracy has been assessed using various measures including the completeness of the description, number of accurate details, number of inaccurate details, and the congruence between the description and the characteristics of the identified suspect.

In a field study addressing this issue, Pigott, Brigham, and Bothwell (1990) had experimenters enter banks in Tallahassee, Florida, and approach tellers to deposit crudely altered money orders. When the tellers refused to cash the money orders, the experimenters became irate and left the bank. Later that day, another experimenter posing as an investigator obtained descriptions and identifications from 47 clerks. The descriptions and identifications were coded for accuracy, completeness, and congruence. Neither description accuracy, completeness, nor congruence correlated significantly with accuracy (the correlations were .03, .09, and .25, respectively). The weak relation between description accuracy and identification accuracy mirrored the results of other studies, as the correlations appear to be positive but small in magnitude (Susa & Meissner, 2008).

Testimony about this factor often works to the detriment of the defendant, because it is the

INFO

The accuracy of a witness's description of a perpetrator is a weak predictor of eyewitness identification accuracy.

defense attorney who would like to argue that the deviation between the witness's description of the perpetrator and the defendant's characteristics suggests that either the witness does not have a good memory of the perpetrator or the defendant is an innocent suspect. The weak relation between description accuracy (or congruence in this instance) suggests that this argument is faulty. For a sample study of the relation between description congruence and identification accuracy, see Wells (1985).

Witness Consistency

Trial practice manuals encourage trial attorneys to elicit inconsistencies in witness testimony and to use these inconsistencies to impeach the witness. In the course of a criminal investigation, a witness will commonly be interviewed numerous times, for example, by the responding officer, investigating officer, and district attorney. Each of these parties may interview the witness more than once. By the time witnesses tell their story in court, they may have described the perpetrator, the events of the crime, and the crime details multiple times. The multiple recounts provide ample data for the defense attorney to mine for inconsistencies.

Fisher and Cutler (1996) reported the results of four separate studies examining the relation between the consistency of eyewitness reports and identification accuracy. Using crime simulation methods, witnesses in each study viewed staged thefts during campus lectures. Each witness provided descriptions of the perpetrators and the event on two separate occasions, and these descriptions were scored for consistency across interviews. Following each set of interviews, each witness attempted to identify the perpetrator from a photoarray, videotaped lineup, or live lineup. In three of the studies, multiple perpetrators were used, so Fisher and Cutler were able to correlate the consistency of descriptions with identification accuracy for eight separate perpetrators. The

INFO

Findings suggest that consistency between a witness's multiple reports is a weak predictor of identification accuracy.

correlations of description consistency with identification accuracy ranged in magnitude from −.04 to .23, and only one was statistically significant. The average correlation was only .10, suggesting that consistency of descriptions is not a good predictor of identification accuracy (Fisher & Cutler, 1996).

We believe that this counterintuitive finding occurs because the consistency of witness recall is strongly influenced by the compatibility of interview, goals, styles, and context from one person to the next and from one situation to the next (Fisher & Cutler, 1996). For example, a witness interviewed at the scene of the crime may be under considerable duress and may also be distracted by other phenomena (e.g., ambient noise at the crime scene, thinking about being late to an appointment), but when interviewed later under less stress and fewer time constraints, the witness may be in a better position to concentrate and may recall more information. As another example, an investigator whose primary motivation is to generate potential leads in the case might encourage the witness to think of as many details as possible without concern about accuracy. By contrast, a district attorney who is attempting to gain closure on the case may encourage witnesses to offer up details about the perpetrator's appearance only if they are certain of their accuracy. These examples of different interview contexts and goals could produce inconsistent reports even if the witness has a very good memory of the crime and perpetrator.

Speed of Identification

In some cases, the witness identifies the perpetrator immediately upon viewing the photoarray. In other cases, the witness ponders over the photoarray and identifies the perpetrator after substantial time has passed. Considerable research has examined the relation between response latency and identification accuracy.

Dunning and Perretta (2002) presented the results of four studies examining the relation between speed of identification and identification accuracy. All of these studies used crime simulation methods. In one study, for example, 201 students viewed a videotaped enactment of a purse snatching at a preschool. The witnesses then gave written descriptions of the events and attempted identifications from perpetrator-present and -absent photoarrays. The identification tests were timed. In all four studies, correct positive identifications were made more quickly than false-positive identifications. Dunning conducted a boundary analysis and concluded that a 10–12 s decision rule best differentiated between accuracy and inaccurate positive identifications; that is, identifications made within 10–12 s were more likely to be correct than those made after a longer period of time. A subsequent analysis of data from over 3,000 witnesses to simulated crimes, however, confirmed that speed of identification was inversely related to accuracy but failed to support the 10–12 s decision rule (Weber, Brewer, Wells, Semmler, & Keast, 2004). The relation between response latency and accuracy for witnesses who rejected their photoarrays, however, was nonsignificant.

The relation between speed of identification and accuracy was also supported in a study of actual crimes (Valentine, Pickering, & Darling, 2003). Valentine and his colleagues studied the predictors of the attempts of over 600 witnesses to identify a perpetrator from lineups conducted by the Metropolitan Police in London. Those witnesses who were labeled by police officers as "fast" choosers were more likely to choose the suspect from the lineup (87%) than were witnesses who the police labeled as "average" or "slow" choosers (38% and 32%, respectively). In contrast, speed of identification decision did not predict witnesses' mistaken choices of lineup fillers (foils). Although these data are limited because it is possible that police officers' labeling of witnesses as fast or slow choosers is influenced by the officers' knowledge of whether the witnesses chose the suspect from the lineup, their consistency with the data from laboratory crime simulation studies suggest that eyewitnesses who make a faster choice from a lineup may be more accurate.

Intervening Identification Tests

Recall from chapter 2 that a good identification test is one that maximizes the chance that the identification can be explained by the witness's original memory of the perpetrator and not by alternative, less diagnostic explanations, such as guessing, deduction, or investigator influence. Another alternative explanation for a positive identification is that the witness recognizes the suspect from an intervening identification test and mistakes the suspect for the perpetrator (a form of transference error; see above). An example of an intervening test is a mugshot procedure. Several studies have examined the impact of intervening mugshot procedures on performance in subsequent identification tests.

Memon, Hope, Bartlett, and Bull (2002) had groups of younger (18–32 years old) and older (60–80 years old) witnesses (169 total) view a crime video. A portion of these witnesses then viewed a book of mugshots; among the mugshots was a critical filler that would appear both in the mugshots and in a photoarray that would be shown to the witness. The remaining witnesses did not look at the book of mugshots. Two days later, all witnesses viewed perpetrator-absent photoarrays that contained the critical filler seen in the mugshots and five new fillers. There were three possible decisions that the witness could make: a correct rejection of the photoarray, an identification of the critical filler who appeared among the previously viewed mugshots, or an identification of one of the new fillers. Witnesses who viewed the mugshot book were more likely to pick the critical filler from the subsequent photoarray than were witnesses who had no mugshot exposure. Witnesses who picked one of the mugshots as the perpetrator's were more likely to choose the previously seen filler from the lineup than witnesses who did not pick a mugshot, irrespective of whether the mugshot they chose in the initial task was the critical filler. Of those who identified any of the mugshots, 40% identified the mugshot that later appeared in the photoarray. Of those who did not make an identification from the mugshots, only 16% identified the filler from the photoarray. Witnesses who mistakenly identified one of the mugshots were more likely to identify the critical filler from the photoarray as the perpetrator. This pattern of effects held whether or not the witness had previously chosen the critical filler during the mugshot task or one of the other mugshots.

3 chapter

In a similar study, Gorenstein and Ellsworth (1980) staged a live event in which a confederate interrupted a psychology class. At the end of the class, half of the students were dismissed and the other half remained and looked at 12 photographs, none of which depicted the perpetrator, to see whether they could identify the confederate from the array. Several days later, participants were shown a photoarray that contained a picture of the confederate. If the participant had been shown the intervening photo array and had incorrectly chosen a photo from that array, that photo was also present in the subsequent array. Forty percent of the participants who had not seen the intervening 12-photoarray chose the confederate whereas only 22% of the participants who had seen the intervening array did so. Moreover, those participants who had chosen someone in the earlier array chose the same person in the subsequent array 44% of the time, a rate that exceeds chance. Behrman and Davey's (2001) study of actual crimes further supports the contention that multiple identification procedures with the same suspect increase the likelihood of suspect identification.

Deffenbacher, Bornstein, and Penrod (2006) conducted a meta-analysis examining the results of 11 articles presenting 32 separate comparisons of the accuracy of identifications made with and without intervening mugshot exposure with over 1,600 witnesses. They found that although mere exposure to mugshots does not affect subsequent identification performance, identifying someone from the mugshots does affect performance on a subsequent photoarray. An innocent suspect is significantly more likely to be identified from a photoarray if the suspect was first identified from a set of mugshots than if there had been no intervening mugshot procedures. This is termed the *mugshot commitment effect* in mugshot research. Commitment effects in mugshot procedures can pose yet another alternative for a positive identification. Some jurisdictions (e.g., New York City) require that a live lineup be conducted even after

INFO

An intervening identification test, such as seeing a mugshot of the suspect, may increase the likelihood that the witness selects the suspect in the subsequent identification tests.

a positive identification of a suspect is obtained using a photoarray. These data suggest that such a practice does not provide useful information about witnesses' memory for the perpetrator as it is possible that when confronted with the live lineup, the witness is picking the suspect because the suspect was previously seen in the initial photoarray and is likely the only person that the lineup and the photoarray have in common.

Admissibility Concepts

General Acceptance

One of the bases for challenging the admissibility of expert testimony is the assertion that the research findings are not generally accepted in the scientific community. In chapter 1 we described some results from surveys of experts conducted by Kassin et al. (1989, 2001). The main purpose of these surveys was to empirically assess the general acceptance of scientific findings concerning the factors that had been reported to influence identification accuracy. In each survey the authors listed a set of factors and provided brief summaries of their purported effects on identification accuracy. Respondents were asked several questions to assess general acceptance as well. For each factor, experts were asked whether the factor was reliable enough for psychologists to present it in courtroom testimony. Eighty percent or more of the experts answered "yes" to this question for the following factors: unconscious transference, presentation format (i.e., simultaneous vs. sequential), exposure time, forgetting curve, accuracy–confidence relation, and weapon focus. Ninety percent or more answered "yes" for the following factors: cross-race bias, alcohol intoxication, mugshot-induced

INFO

Challenges to admissibility of expert testimony on eyewitness research include

- whether the research findings are generally accepted in the scientific community
- whether the substantive content of the expert testimony is within the ken of the average juror
- whether expert testimony results in prejudicial impact and juror confusion

INFO

The high rates of agreement among experts about many eyewitness factors (see text) support the conclusion that findings in the eyewitness research are generally accepted in the relevant scientific community.

bias, confidence malleability, and lineup instructions. Several additional findings are noteworthy. Showups met with slightly lower levels of general acceptance (74% answered "yes" to the reliability question). The description for showups was "the use of a one-person showup instead of a full lineup increases the risk of misidentification." The lower levels of agreement probably reflect the relative dearth of research on this topic (Steblay et al., 2003). Regardless of the rates of false identifications from showups versus lineups, there should be less disagreement with the notion that showups provide less protection than lineups against identification due to guessing, deduction, and investigator influence. The other noteworthy finding is that the level of stress experienced by the witness also met with lower levels of general acceptance (60% answered "yes" to the reliability question for stress). This survey, however, was conducted before the publication of two influential articles: the aforementioned meta-analysis of the effects of stress (Deffenbacher et al., 2004) and the field study (Morgan et al., 2004). We suspect that higher levels of consensus now exist.

Common Sense

Perhaps the most common basis for challenging the admissibility of expert testimony is the assertion that the substantive content of the expert testimony is within the ken of the average juror and therefore expert testimony is not needed to assist the jury. Are jurors of their own accord knowledgeable about the factors that influence identification accuracy? When evaluating eyewitness identifications, do they rely upon factors known from the research to actually influence identification accuracy and ignore or rely less upon factors known from the research to be weak predictors of identification accuracy? A large body of research has been brought data to bear on these questions, much of which was summarized by Cutler and Penrod (1995). Surveys of prospective jurors from around the United States and in other countries reveal substantial gaps in lay knowledge about the factors that influence eyewitness identification. In one large-scale survey, for example, Schmechel, O'Toole, Easterly, and Loftus (2006) surveyed 1,007 jury-eligible citizens in the Washington DC area for their knowledge about the factors that influence eyewitness identification. They found that substantial percentages of respondents lacked understanding of how factors such as weapon focus, cross-race recognition, stress, and suggestive identification procedures impact identification accuracy and also misunderstood the relation between eyewitness confidence and identification accuracy.

Researchers have also used trial simulation methodology to examine jurors' evaluations of eyewitness identification testimony. The results of these studies suggest that jurors (both college students and jury-eligible citizens) ignore factors that are known to influence identification accuracy (e.g., Cutler, Penrod, & Dexter, 1990) and rely heavily on factors that are known to be weak predictors of identification accuracy, such as confidence at the time of trial and the consistency of identification testimony (see Cutler & Penrod, 1995). For example, Cutler et al. (1990) reported the results of a trial simulation experiment involving 450 students and jury-eligible community members. The mock jurors viewed videotapes of a robbery trial that hinged on eyewitness identification. The conditions surrounding the crime and the identification were systematically manipulated, and their effects on jurors' evaluations of the identification and trial outcome were examined. Factors such as violence of the crime, weapon presence, whether a disguise was worn by the perpetrator, retention interval, and suggestive identification procedures were expected to but did not significantly influence mock-juror judgments. The only factor that systematically influenced juror judgments was the confidence of the eyewitness. This study supported the assertion that jurors are not sensitive to the factors known from research to affect the accuracy of eyewitness identification and instead rely on a factor—witness confidence—that is only weakly correlated with witness accuracy. In addition, several studies show that mock jurors are unable to distinguish accurate from inaccurate witnesses at rates that exceed guessing (e.g., Lindsay, Wells, & O'Connor, 1989).

Another source of evidence that the research findings are beyond the ken of the average juror is the reforms that have been enacted in several states and many police departments. Many police departments have adopted—and others are planning to adopt—reforms that have emerged from the research, such as standard admonitions, sequentially presented lineups, and double-blind procedures (Wells, 2006). If jurors were aware of the problems produced by biased lineup instructions, simultaneous presentation, and nonblind procedures, then there may be no need to enact the reforms because they could appropriately weight an identification based on the quality of the procedures used to produce it.

Prejudicial Impact and Confusion

Some courts have raised concerns that expert testimony may prejudice or confuse the jury. In an effort to empirically examine this concern, several investigators have conducted trial simulation research to examine the impact of expert testimony on juror decisions. In these trial simulation studies, mock jurors (students or jury-eligible community members) watch a simulated trial (transcript or videotaped enactment) including the testimony of an eyewitness. The investigators manipulate the presence or absence of expert testimony and may also manipulate the conditions surrounding the crime or identification.

Some of the earlier studies using this methodology tended to show that expert testimony made jurors more skeptical about the accuracy of eyewitness identification (Leippe, 1995). Several earlier studies (e.g., Cutler, Dexter, & Penrod, 1989; Cutler, Penrod, & Dexter, 1989; Devenport, Stinson, Cutler, & Kravitz, 2002) found that expert testimony improved juror sensitivity to factors known from the research to affect identification accuracy and reduced jurors' reliance on eyewitness confidence. More recent studies have found relatively weak effects for expert testimony. Devenport and Cutler

INFO

No evidence currently exists that jurors are confused or unduly prejudiced by expert testimony on eyewitness research.

(2004), for example, found no effect for expert testimony, and Leippe, Eisendstadt, Rauch, and Seib (2004) found that expert testimony influenced juror skepticism only when the judge reminded the jurors about the expert.

In sum, although the research is rather mixed concerning the influence of expert testimony on juror decisions, there is no research showing that jurors are confused or prejudiced by it. One might claim that the finding that jurors are made skeptical by expert testimony is a form of prejudice, but this is debatable because enhanced skepticism would be warranted in those studies to the extent that the conditions surrounding the crime and identification would increase the likelihood of false identification.

3
chapter

APPLICATION

Preparation for the Evaluation

4

G iven that the main point of expert testimony in this context is to educate the judge and jury about the scientific research on eyewitness memory, getting prepared for an evaluation requires staying current with the psychological literature on eyewitness memory. As evidenced by the number of journal publications, books, book chapters, and conference presentations that appear each year, the research field of eyewitness memory is quite active. Staying current with original research involves regularly consulting journals in which eyewitness research is published, such as *Law and Human Behavior*, *Applied Cognitive Psychology*, *Journal of Experimental Psychology: Applied*, *Journal of Applied Social Psychology*, and *Psychology, Crime, and Law*. Eyewitness research is also regularly presented at conferences such as the annual American Psychology-Law Society conference.

When contacted with a potential opportunity to testify, preparation for the evaluation can be considered as having two phases: *initial consultation* and *guiding discovery*. Initial consultation refers to the exchange between the attorney and expert and addresses issues such as whether the expert has the relevant expertise; what are the expert's qualifications, experience, and availability; and whether the expert will be able to be helpful given the fact pattern of the specific case. In guiding discovery, the expert reviews the case materials assembled by the attorney and may assist in the development of additional case materials.

BEST PRACTICE

Keep abreast of current research on eyewitness memory.

Initial Consultation

Preparation for evaluation begins early—from the initial moment that an attorney calls the eyewitness expert to inquire about his services. There are typically three common elements to the initial consultation: assessment of expertise, availability, and cost. A fourth element, previewing the case, occurs in some cases but not in others. Previewing the case happens when the attorney provides some basic details about the crime that was committed, allowing the expert to develop a general idea about whether the fact pattern contains characteristics that research suggests affect eyewitness accuracy. The attorney might explain, by phone or e-mail, the conditions under which the crime occurred and the nature of the identification test. We call this portion of the initial consultation a "preview" because it is prior to the review of the actual case discovery and often the attorney does not cover all of the relevant factors in her summary of the case facts.

Initial consultation typically begins with an e-mail message or a telephone call from an attorney or an attorney's assistant in search of an eyewitness expert. Sometimes the attorney provides some initial information about the case. In the authors' experiences, most attorneys who contact eyewitness experts are doing so for the first time; they have little familiarity with eyewitness expert testimony, and they do not know the experts. Attorneys find experts through a variety of means, including referrals from other attorneys, listservs, expert lists maintained by bar associations and academies, and referrals from other eyewitness experts who have declined the case because of time constraints. Attorneys also find experts by searching the literature and contacting authors of studies.

INFO

Elements to Initial Consultation:

1. Assessment of expertise
2. Availability
3. Cost
4. Previewing the case (optional)

Assessment of Expertise

Because attorneys are often contacting experts whom they do not know and with whom they have not previously worked, it is not uncommon for attorneys to ask experts whether they have expertise on eyewitness memory and whether they provide expert testimony. Some attorneys will ask for additional details concerning the expert's qualifications, including whether they have conducted research in the area. Usually, attorneys will ask to see a copy of the expert's curriculum vitae. The attorneys might interview experts about the extent of their experience testifying in court and the states or counties in which they have testified. Attorneys might ask for references in the form of names and contact information of attorneys for whom the expert has testified in previous cases. The attorney might ask experts about their style of testimony and ask questions of sufficient depth that the attorney can assess the potential expert's patience, verbal demeanor, and ability to articulate complex concepts. The procedure can begin to feel like a job interview. In our experience, however, the degree of preemployment screening is minimal, particularly when the attorney learns that the expert has a lot of experience. Here is an example of a typical initial inquiry received by the authors:

Hello Dr. Cutler/Kovera,

I am looking for an identification expert for a criminal case that I have scheduled in the Circuit Court for [county and state], that begins on [date]. I got your name from [name], another lawyer in my office. She had retained you last year to testify in a case of hers, but Judge [name] excluded the testimony after taking a proffer. The case was [case name]. She says that you were great.

My case, [case name] involves a Hispanic victim of an attempted armed robbery at night by three Black guys. One guy held a shotgun, one held a knife. Police showed the victim a photographic array three months after the attack, and picked my client out. I have no idea why they waited three months.

I have not gotten authorization from the Public Defender Headquarters in [state] to retain you yet, but I wanted to check your availability first. The case should last two days, and I could possibly get the Court to agree to let you testify on the [date] if I arrange it in advance. Are you available and interested? Please advise.

4
chapter

Availability

As the above inquiry illustrates, once expertise is established or confirmed, the conversation may turn to availability. Availability becomes an issue if there is a trial scheduled. Sometimes, attorneys contact expert witnesses on short notice (e.g., for a trial in a week or two), in which case availability becomes a critical issue. Other times the proceeding is at a nascent stage, and there is no trial date on the horizon. Other times there is a trial date scheduled, but the attorney expresses confidence that the trial date can be postponed if needed (a regular occurrence in this business). Sometimes the attorney is seeking only consultation and anticipates an eventual plea bargain. In these cases, the attorney may be trying to assess the strength of the client's case and may use the threat of expert testimony as part of the plea bargaining strategy.

Cost

With availability established, the topic of the exchange typically turns to fees and expenses. The attorney may want to know the expert's hourly fee, the projected total fee, and the projected total expenses (mainly travel expenses). In the authors' experiences, most attorneys who seek expert testimony are representing indigent clients. The attorneys are either public defenders or private attorneys appointed by an indigent defense agency. In these cases, the attorneys must seek approval from their respective agencies for expert fees. In the case in which the attorney was retained with private funds, often the attorney must seek approval from the private funding source for the expert fees. It is important to provide realistic estimates, because the courts and indigent defense agencies approve a maximum amount of funding and are not receptive to invoices that exceed the amounts approved. If the expert finds at any point that the approved funds are insufficient, additional funds should be requested before the trial. Sometimes, attorneys ask how much time and funding is needed just to review discovery and consult with them about the expert's evaluation of the discovery materials and will request only the funds needed to cover these initial expenses. If, following

BEST PRACTICE

Provide realistic estimates of total fees and expenses for the case, so that the attorney can secure the appropriate funding.

consultation, the attorney decides that expert testimony would be helpful, the attorney requests more funding at that time.

Previewing the Case

Sometimes, initial consultation only focuses on the topics summarized above: expertise, availability, costs, and relevant discovery. In these cases, the attorney expects the expert to become familiar with some of the facts of the case before they discuss the expert's potential contribution as an expert witness. In other cases, however, the attorney prefers to preview the case for the expert and to make an initial determination of whether expert testimony is worth pursuing. Both approaches are reasonable, but each has risks and benefits.

The benefit of the preview approach is that it can save time and money. Many cases are not well-suited for expert testimony. For example, if the conditions surrounding the crime were favorable for witnessing and the eyewitness knew the perpetrator, expert testimony is unlikely to help and could hurt the defendant's case. In cases like this, the expert might readily conclude that this is not a favorable situation for offering expert testimony, explain the rationale to the attorney, and decline the invitation without further review. Another benefit of the preview approach is that the expert can explain to the attorney the typical scope of expert testimony and dispel any misconceptions that the attorney might have. As mentioned above, most attorneys are not familiar with this form of expertise and have not worked with an eyewitness expert in a previous case. One misconception sometimes held by attorneys is that the expert believes (based on the scientific research) that eyewitnesses are usually wrong and that the expert will convey this fact to the jury. The expert should explain to the attorney that the purpose of expert testimony is to educate the jury about general principles associated with memory and to explain the factors that are known from the research to influence the accuracy of eyewitness identification. The expert will offer no opinion about the accuracy of the specific eyewitness nor offer an opinion that eyewitnesses to crimes are usually

4
chapter

BEWARE
The attorney may expect an expert to opine on the accuracy of the specific eyewitness or that eyewitnesses to crimes are usually incorrect.

incorrect. Offering such explanations may lead the attorney to conclude that expert testimony will not help her case and may obviate the need for further review of discovery.

The risk associated with previewing the case is that the attorney might inadvertently misrepresent or omit case facts and thus provide a misleading preview. The main risk in this instance is prematurely and incorrectly concluding that expert testimony is not likely to be helpful in this case and declining the opportunity. This risk is substantial, because many attorneys are not familiar with the research base and do not know the factors that the expert will look for in evaluating the discovery. For example, the authors have had cases in which the attorneys initially focus on general impairment factors but do not raise some suspect bias factors that are important, such as simultaneous presentation and nonblind lineups. Concluding, based on a case preview, that expert testimony would not be helpful in a case is a risk because the decision is unlikely to be revisited, and there is therefore little chance to correct it. Prematurely and incorrectly concluding that expert testimony would be beneficial is less of a risk at this stage, because the decision can easily be revisited and corrected following review of discovery and subsequent consultation.

Guiding Discovery

Guiding discovery involves setting the parameters for expert testimony and obtaining the relevant material for review.

Setting the Parameters

It is important that, very early in the review process, the expert clearly convey to the attorney the scope and limits of expert testimony, particularly given that most attorneys are new to this form of expert testimony. It is important to communicate to the attorney that the main thrust of the expert testimony will be to educate the jury about memory processes generally and about how specific factors are known from research to influence identification accuracy. Another purpose is to dispel myths about eyewitness memory. It is as important to convey that the expert will not offer an opinion about the accuracy of the eyewitness in the case or offer hypothetical opinions that would suggest to the jury that the expert believes the eyewitness to be inaccurate. The reasoning behind these admonitions is that the science underlying expert testimony, as reviewed in chapter 3, is not sufficiently advanced to permit the accurate assessment of individual witnesses. The attorney cannot be expected to know the relevant science and its limitations and may therefore express surprise that the expert will not be in a position to offer an opinion about the witness's accuracy or respond to a hypothetical question and eyewitness accuracy. Given that the attorney must ultimately decide whether the expert's testimony will be helpful in the case, it is important to clearly explain the scope and limits of the expert testimony before you begin your review of the relevant discovery data.

BEST PRACTICE

Clearly explain to the attorney the scope and limits of expert testimony on the psychology of eyewitness identification.

Obtaining Relevant Materials

The second task in the preparation for review involves determining what discovery materials will be needed for the expert's review. The attorney typically asks experts what they need to see. We recommend that the expert request all information pertaining to (a) the conditions under which the crime occurred and (b) the identification of the defendant. This information should include all police reports of the incident, witness statements, photoarrays (usually photocopies), and photoarray instructions. In states in which attorneys are permitted to depose witnesses and police investigators, the expert should obtain deposition transcripts. Other potentially useful information include transcripts of the grand jury hearing or motions to suppress identifications (particularly if either includes testimony from eyewitnesses or investigators). Attorneys often simply photocopy and send all information in their files. It is important for the expert to be proactive in seeking discovery information.

BEST PRACTICE

Request from the attorney all information pertaining to

1. the conditions under which the crime occurred and
2. the identification of the defendant.

4
chapter

Attorneys will normally send any information they have in the file, but they may not know what additional information will be helpful to the expert.

The expert should feel comfortable in asking for additional information, even if this means that the attorney must take action to obtain the information. For example, sometimes an attorney will indicate that there were multiple eyewitnesses to the crime, but the prosecution is proffering the testimony of one eyewitness or a subset of the available eyewitnesses. The attorney has the reports from to-be-proffered witnesses and sends them to the expert, but has no information on the other witnesses. The attorney may only be concerned with the witness who is planning to testify and so she does not pursue the reports of the other witnesses. Reports of the other witnesses, however, may be useful to the expert, so the expert should ask the attorney to request the reports of the other witnesses. In our experience, attorneys are glad to oblige with such requests and appreciate the expert guidance. The expert should not be concerned with burdening the attorney. In some cases (e.g., capital cases, where the attorney has a more substantive budget for planning the defense), the attorney has hired a private investigator and makes the investigator available for the expert's needs. Other attorneys have law clerks that assist with these tasks. Attorneys who work solo make the time to fulfill the expert's reasonable requests.

Review of discovery can be a continuous rather than a discrete process, depending on the stage in the proceeding at which the expert is initially engaged. If the expert is engaged relatively late in the process, for example, a couple of weeks before the trial or to provide an affidavit to be used in an appeal, then the attorney's discovery process may be relatively complete, and the expert can be presented with a full set of information for review. This full set of information might include police reports; witness statements; transcripts of witness interviews, the indictment hearing, the motion-to-suppress hearing, and depositions with the eyewitnesses and investigators; and a photoarray and accompanying instructions. Sometimes, in contrast, the expert is engaged very early in the process when discovery is still in process. In these cases, the expert might initially receive only the police reports and a copy of the photoarray. The expert in these cases can be helpful in providing guidance to the attorney about what information is needed. Indeed, it is most helpful when the expert has the opportunity to have input into discovery. For example, the expert can suggest questions for the attorney to ask the eyewitnesses and investigators in interviews, depositions, and during suppression hearings. Both authors have had such opportunities. Some experts have also assisted the attorney with preparing direct and cross-examination questions for witnesses at trial when the judge did not allow expert testimony. In several cases, the experts were invited to submit questions to the attorney to be asked of the witness and the investigator during a suppression hearing. These questions are designed to extract as much information as possible from both sources about general impairment and suspect bias factors that may have been present during the witnessing of the crime or the subsequent investigation of the crime, including interviews of the witness that may have suggested new information to the witness or suggestive identification procedures.

In cases in which the expert has a role in guiding discovery, the expert's goal should be a complete understanding of the conditions under which the perpetrator was witnessed and the conditions under which an identification was produced. With respect to the witnessing conditions, in chapter 3 we presented a long list of factors that should be assessed for their presence, absence, or levels. For example, the expert should seek data about the races of the witness and perpetrator, the level of stress experienced by the witness, the opportunity for weapon focus, any disguises worn by the perpetrator, and other such factors affecting the opportunity to observe the perpetrator. Police reports can also be reviewed to determine whether witness descriptions of crime perpetrator changed over time.

BEST PRACTICE

When having a role in guiding discovery, seek information about the following:

- general impairment factors
- suspect bias factors
- postdictors of identification accuracy
- other witnessing and identification factors that are relevant to the case

4
chapter

We also presented in chapter 3 the factors that affect the likelihood of correct and mistaken identification in an identification test, and these factors should provide guidance for discovery as well. For example, the expert should find out whether there were standard instructions given prior to the photoarray (and obtain a copy), the logic behind the choice of fillers (PDM or SM), how the photoarray was presented (simultaneous or sequential presentation), and whether the investigator who conducted the identification test knew the identity of the suspect during the test (i.e., double-blind administration). If the photoarray was shown to the witness in color, the expert should obtain a color copy for inspection. The expert should also attempt to ascertain whether there were factors present that could lead to confidence inflation, such as confirmatory feedback provided to the witness by the investigator after the witness made a positive identification but before the witness expressed his level of confidence in the accuracy of that identification. Documentation on these issues varies from police department to police department, but there is almost always a photocopy of the photoarray in the file. Although the file will likely indicate whether the witness looked at mugshots, it is less likely that there will be documentation of which mugshots were shown to a witness. If there was a standard set of written instructions, it is usually in the file. If instructions are not standard, it may be possible that pretrial testimony from the witness or an investigating officer will detail their reports of what was said before the identification procedure. Other aspects of the procedure (e.g., type of presentation and double-blind administration) can be ascertained from the discovery materials, but in cases in which it is not clear, the expert should ask the attorney to find out this information.

The factors listed in chapter 3, however, should not be considered exhaustive. Indeed, chapter 3 is limited to factors for which there is substantial empirical research. There may be witnessing and identification factors that are relevant to discovery and expert testimony that may not have been discussed in chapter 3 because they have not been subjected to research. The expert must therefore approach the task with an open mind and be prepared to identify the complete context in which the crime was witnessed and the identification produced.

Ethical Issues in Providing Eyewitness Expert Testimony

Psychologists who provide expert testimony should be knowledgeable about and adhere to ethical principles governing their work.

Ethical Principles for Psychologists and Code of Conduct

The APA adopted the *Ethical Principles for Psychologists and Code of Conduct* in 2002 (the original principles were published in 1953 and have been revised several times since then). Most of the APA's guidelines pertain to psychological training, assessment, and treatment, but some of these principles are also relevant to expert testimony about eyewitness memory—or about any such topic.

Section 2 of the *Principles* pertains to competence and states that psychologists must practice within their boundaries of competence, undertake relevant education and training, and become familiar with the judicial rules governing their roles. They must undertake ongoing efforts to maintain their competence and ensure their work is based on established scientific knowledge of their discipline. They must refrain from activity when personal problems prevent them (or can be expected to prevent them) from performing competently. As the science of eyewitness memory continues to develop at a fairly rapid pace, it is important that experts on eyewitness issues continue to familiarize themselves with new research in the area and be able to recognize when the science does not address a particular issue raised by a case or the validity of an argument that an attorney wishes to pursue.

4
chapter

INFO

Ethical issues for expert witnesses include

- competence
- conflict of interest
- confidentiality
- financial arrangements
- knowledge of scientific research and its limits
- consistency with professional and legal standards

Under the Human Relations category, psychologists must avoid conflicts of interest. Expert witnesses typically receive confidential documents through discovery. Principle 4.01 reminds psychologists of their obligation to protect confidential information. Expert testimony is a form of public statement, and therefore Section 5 of the *Principles* is relevant. Section 5 specifies that psychologists must not make false or deceptive statements about their research, credentials, or degrees. When speaking with reporters, psychologists must ensure that their comments are based on knowledge, training, or experience and are consistent with the *Principles*.

Expert witnesses typically receive remuneration for their time, making relevant the ethical principles associated with fees and financial arrangements (Section 6). These principles dictate that psychologists and the parties retaining them early on reach agreement concerning financial arrangements, set fees that are consistent with law, do not misrepresent their fees, and discuss early on the limitations to services that could result from limitations in financing.

Specialty Guidelines for Forensic Psychologists

As mentioned earlier, the APA principles apply to a wide range of professional activity in which psychologists engage. In 1991, the journal *Law and Human Behavior* published *Specialty Guidelines for Forensic Psychologists*. These guidelines were developed and endorsed by the American Psychology-Law Society (Division 41, APA) and the American Academy of Forensic Psychology and are currently under revision. These principles are relevant to the work of psychologists who testify as expert witnesses in a variety of domains, including eyewitness identification.

Section 2 of the *Guidelines* specifies that forensic psychologists maintain the highest standards of their profession and take efforts to ensure that their services are used in a forthright and responsible manner. Section 3, pertaining to competence, specifies that forensic psychologists practice within the boundaries of their education and training, present details of their training and education in court, understand the legal standards and procedures for expert testimony, and decline participation in cases in which their own values interfere with their performance.

Section 4 of the principles concerns relationships. This section describes the responsibilities of psychologists during initial consultation, including fee setting, conveying potential conflicts of interest, explaining the limits of competence and the limits of the scientific base on which the expert will be relying. This section also reminds psychologists to avoid conflicts of interest (e.g., personal relationships with parties that are inconsistent with the anticipated professional relationship) and to fully disclose conflicts that arise during professional service. Section 5 addresses the need to protect confidentiality of records and pertains to discovery provided by the attorney to the expert and any correspondence and reports.

Section 6 of the *Guidelines* pertains to methods and procedures. In this section, the expert is reminded to stay current in scientific knowledge and be prepared to document (including in court) the evidence and data relied upon. When psychologists are called upon to make public statements, Section 7 specifies that they must promote understanding, take steps to correct misuse or misrepresentation of their testimony, provide information that is consistent with professional and legal standards, and represent professional disagreements (e.g., with opposing experts) fairly and accurately. Generally, according to the *Guidelines*, psychologists should avoid public statements, but when they do give public statements, they should stick to what is available in the public record. Last, psychologists are aware that their own judgments and opinions must be distinguished from legal facts, opinions, and conclusions. They must be prepared to explain the relationship between their expert testimony and legal issues in the cases in which they work.

4
chapter

Data Collection | 5

The expert's review of the relevant discovery is a straightforward process. The expert is assessing the presence, absence, and levels of the general impairment factors, suspect bias factors, and postdictors that have established relationships (or nonrelationships) with identification accuracy, as reviewed in chapter 3. For example, the expert documents whether the identification was cross-race, the amount of stress experienced by the witness, the visual presence of a weapon, and so on. The expert also documents the photoarray procedures, such as the instructions used, the manner in which fillers were selected, and the procedures for presenting the photos to the witness. The expert further documents the postdictors, such as the confidence expressed by the witness and any factors that might have led to confidence inflation.

Process of Data Collection

The expert's data collection is normally limited to the documentation, including the police reports, witness statements, and, if available, transcripts of hearings involving the witness and investigator (e.g., indictment hearing, motions to suppress, witness depositions). The expert typically does not have direct contact with the witness or investigator and does not visit the crime scene.

Reasons to Not Contact the Witness

The expert does not have direct contact with the eyewitness for several reasons. First, it is usually not needed. The expert's role is to assess levels of general impairment factors, suspect bias factors, and postdictors. Information about these factors can normally be obtained without contacting the witness. For example, police reports and witness statements typically provide perpetrator descriptions and indicate the presence of disguises (e.g., whether the perpetrator was wearing a hat or scarf). The visual presence of a weapon can usually be ascertained from these reports. The races of the witness and perpetrator are usually in the police reports, but if they are not, the attorney can obtain the information. Stress experienced by the witness may be commented upon by the witness in her statement ("I was terrified"), by the investigator in his report ("it took a while to interview the witness because she was very shaken by the event"), or by medical personnel who examine the witness, or can be inferred from listening to tapes of the witness reporting the crime to 911. Thus, one reason for not interviewing the witness is that it is often not necessary, and doing what is not necessary is a waste of time and money when a consulting fee is involved.

Another reason for not interviewing a witness is to avoid influencing the witness or the appearance of having influenced the witness. We know from eyewitness research that witnesses are susceptible to social influence, so why risk influencing the witness's testimony (or the appearance of doing so)? A third reason for not interviewing the witness is that the expert is not assessing the witness. Recall that the expert will offer no opinion about the accuracy of the witness but rather will focus her expert testimony on general impairment factors, suspect bias factors, and postdictors of identification accuracy. A fourth reason for not interviewing the witness is that the witness may not be a good source of information about general impairment factors, suspect bias factors, and postdictors. Witnesses may be predisposed against cooperating with the defense, and that includes both the defense attorney and the defense expert witnesses. Witnesses are not under oath during interviews. By the time the expert becomes involved, considerable time may have elapsed following the crime, and the passage of time and other intervening factors may have influenced the witness's recollection for the relevant factors. Information taken soon after the crime, such as that contained in police reports and in witness statements, should be a more valid source of information about the relevant factors.

We can think of only one valid reason for interviewing a witness, and that is so that the expert can answer "yes" when the prosecuting attorney, on cross-examination, asks, "Did you interview the witness in this case?" Admittedly,

this is not a very compelling reason. Although answering yes may allow the expert to avoid a line of cross-examination in which the opposing counsel attempts to undermine the credibility of the expert by insinuating that the expert has nothing of use to tell the jury if he did not speak to the witness, we feel it is better to inoculate jurors against this argument by addressing why the expert did not interview the witness during the expert's direct testimony. Underscoring the expert's role as an educator on eyewitness factors and noting to the jury that it is her role to discern the credibility of the eyewitness usually deflates the prosecutor's attack about not having interviewed the witness.

Reasons to Not Contact the Investigator

For some of the same reasons, it is atypical to interview the investigator who conducted the identification test. Much of the information the expert is capable of learning is in the police reports, and the attorney should be able to fill in the gaps. Clearly, there is more information that the expert should know, such as the precise nature of the interaction between the investigator and witness before and during the identification test. The expert is on the lookout for potential suggestive influences. Research suggests that the investigator, however, will not be a good source of information about these influences, with research on the effects of single-blind lineup administration on witness accuracy providing evidence that neither administrators nor witnesses are aware of biases that may be exhibited by the administrator (Greathouse & Kovera, 2009). Thus, if investigators subtly and inadvertently influenced witnesses, they would probably not be aware of it. If investigators obviously and advertently influenced witnesses, they probably would not admit to doing so. If the information was not documented and considerable time has passed, the investigator may not recall a lot of detail about the identification procedure.

5
chapter

Cases of Limited Documentation

In some cases the amount of documentation available from the witness and investigator may be limited. Limited documentation is possible in states in which discovery laws are minimal and in cases in which documentation practices were not carefully followed. The witness may not have been asked to produce a written statement, and the police reports may be lacking in critical detail. The witness may have refused to cooperate with the defense attorney. In these cases, the defense attorney may learn relevant details about the general impairment and suspect bias factors in real time, as the trial is progressing. The defense attorney then has a relatively short period of time to brief the expert, and the expert likewise has a short period of time to formulate any new opinions concerning the relevant factors. This briefing could occur in a meeting or telephone conversation the evening before the expert is scheduled to testify, or it could occur during a trial break.

In some of these cases, the judge, at the request of the defense attorney, will waive the *sequestration rule* (requiring that witnesses not hear one another's testimony) and allow the expert to hear the testimony of the eyewitness and investigator. For this to happen, however, the expert must be willing and available to attend these aspects of the hearing. These situations are relatively rare because judges are reluctant to waive the sequestration rule (particularly at the objection of the prosecution) and the expert may not have the extra day or more needed to attend the trial. When they do occur, however, they provide an excellent opportunity for the expert to hear sworn testimony about the relevant factors. It is usually not possible to review transcripts of the witness or investigator testimony before the expert testifies. As eyewitness experts are most typically called to testify in robbery cases that typically last 1 to 3 days, it is almost impossible to obtain a transcript of the relevant testimony in time for the expert to review it before testifying. When testimony is available it is usually from pretrial hearings to suppress the identification.

Empirical Evaluation of the Photoarray

In cases in which the defense maintains that the photoarray was significantly biased against the defendant and the expert shares this view, the expert may wish to conduct an empirical evaluation of the photoarray. The methodology for empirical assessment involves use of the "mock-witness paradigm" (see Buckhout, Rabinowitz, Alfonso, Kanellis, & Anderson, 1988, for an example of its use). A sample of individuals who did not witness the crime and do not know the perpetrator or suspect (called mock witnesses) are provided the description of the perpetrator given by the witness and asked to identify which photo is of the suspect (Doob & Kirshenbaum, 1973). In theory, an unbiased lineup is one in which the suspect should not be chosen at levels greater than chance by a mock witnesses. If the suspect is chosen at a level greater than chance, it must be due to suspect bias factors associated with the composition of the photoarray. For example, if the suspect's photo is the only photo that matches the description of the perpetrator, the mock witnesses should disproportionately identify the suspect as the best match to the perpetrator. If this happens, the expert would be on firm ground in opining that the photoarray is biased against the suspect. A witness who remembers his description will be able to identify the suspect, even if he has no memory of the perpetrator. In the framework we presented for understanding positive identifications in chapter 2, identification by deduction would be a compelling alternative explanation for the witness's positive identification of the suspect.

5
chapter

Indices of Lineup Fairness

Several indices exist for quantifying the fairness of the composition of photoarrays (the November 1999 issue of *Applied Cognitive Psychology* is devoted to the topic of measuring lineup fairness). One measure of lineup fairness is called the functional size of the lineup, which provides an index of how many lineup members are plausible picks from the lineup given the description of the perpetrator. This index is obtained by dividing the number of mock witnesses by the number of suspect identifications (Wells, Leippe, & Ostrom, 1979). For example, if 16 of 40 mock witnesses (40%) identify the suspect, then the lineup has a functional size of 2.50 no matter how many foils the lineup contains. Effective size (Malpass, Tredoux, & McQuiston-Surrett, 2007) and E' (Tredoux, 1998) are other measures of lineup fairness.

Advantages and Limited Opportunities

The empirical assessment of photoarrays has many advantages. Such assessments give the expert the opportunity to offer more than general opinions about the research, for they allow the expert to offer opinions about the photoarray in the case. Although an expert can offer an opinion without the empirical assessment, an opinion following empirical assessment is more defensible and should be more compelling. There is no question that composition bias can be a problem in actual cases, as has been exhibited in a number of studies in which mock-witness paradigms have been used to assess the fairness of actual lineups. These studies have generally tested the fairness of lineups whose fairness had already been contested during the course of a case (Brigham, Meissner, & Wasserman, 1999; Wells & Bradfield, 1999), but there is at least one study in which researchers tested a representative sample of lineups and also found composition bias (Valentine & Heaton, 1999). Nevertheless, the opportunities to conduct empirical assessments of composition bias are limited for several reasons. Investigators can be quite capable of selecting fillers that closely match description of either the the perpetrator or the suspect. In many of our cases, we look over the photoarray and conclude that there are no major problems with the composition. In cases in which there are very obvious problems with composition, empirical assessment may not be needed to make the point. Second, even when lineup composition appears to be a problem, it may be difficult to convince attorneys to spend the extra money for a mock-witness assessment of lineup fairness, especially when they believe that they can make a compelling case for biased lineup composition during their closing arguments.

Interpretation | 6

A t some point before the trial, experts will have all of the information they need to formulate their opinions and, together with the defense attorney, plan their expert testimony. The point at which this occurs may vary as a function of the discovery issues discussed earlier. The interpretation process is relatively straightforward. The facts of the case should be compared against two data sources: the research literature concerning the factors that influence identification accuracy and best practices in identification tests. Once this interpretation is complete, the expert discusses this assessment with the attorney and discusses whether expert testimony should be offered in the case.

Comparing Case Facts Against the Research Literature

The basic question asked in this analysis is which well-established factors are relevant to this case? The set of discovery should be mined for the relevant general impairment factors, suspect bias factors, and postdictors. To make this task easier, we recommend that the expert create a checklist or form in advance of review. This form would list all of the potential factors (such as those listed in chapter 3) and leave space for detailed notes.

For example, in the section concerning general impairment factors, there would be entries for estimated exposure time, the race of the

BEST PRACTICE

Compare case facts against both

- the research literature and
- best practices in identification tests.

witness, any disguises worn by the perpetrator, the race of the perpetrator, the presence of a weapon, and notes about stress experienced by the witness.

In the section for suspect bias factors, there would be entries for number of photos, the expert's impression of the composition of the photoarray, the presence of standard instructions, the quality of the instructions if present, the manner in which the photos were presented (simultaneously or sequentially), and whether the investigator conducting the photoarray was blind to the identity of the suspect at the time of the identification procedure.

The section of the form concerning postdictors would include entries for the witness's confidence in her identification, notes about how and when witness's confidence was assessed and any factors that might have influenced the witness's confidence level (e.g., confirmatory feedback by the investigator), speed of the identification, and other postdictors. For each factor, we also recommend noting the source and page number of the relevant information for ease of reference during subsequent review of the discovery, discussions with the attorney, or use at trial.

Completing a form like the one described above should give the expert a comprehensive picture of the relevant factors. This picture will be helpful in conveying both the strengths and the weaknesses to the defense attorney as part of any oral or written report and for the purpose of planning direct examination.

Comparing Case Facts Against Best Practices

The task here is similar to that just described for comparing the case facts with the research literature but here the goal is to compare the identification procedure with existing sets of best practices. Whether the identification test was a showup, photoarray, or live lineup, the procedures vary, and written guidelines now exist for minimizing bias in each type of identification test. One such set of best practices is the U.S. Department of Justice's *Eyewitness evidence: A guide for law enforcement* (U.S. Department of Justice, 1999). Several states, including New Jersey and North Carolina, have adopted new guidelines for collecting eyewitness identification evidence. Reform is in progress in other states as well.

BEST PRACTICE

Be familiar with best-practice guidelines for collecting eyewitness identification evidence.

Comparing the procedures used to best practices serves several purposes. First, the best practices provide useful benchmarks for the jury. Second, the existence of guidelines and the reform movement confirm that the psychological research and the opinions of the expert are relevant and accepted within some law enforcement communities. Third, the guidelines mute the criticism that the research upon which the expert's opinion is based does not generalize to actual crimes, a point sometimes raised during cross-examination. The best-practice guidelines were based in large measure on the psychological research and are summarized as follows:

Department of Justice: Best Practices in Identification Tests

The best-practice literature on identification tests has evolved over time. The first government agency to produce a set of best practices was the Department of Justice. A panel of attorneys, police officers, and psychologists convened by Attorney General Janet Reno produced the document entitled *Eyewitness evidence: A guide for law enforcement* (U.S. Department of Justice, 1999). This guide addresses the collection and preservation of eyewitness evidence from police interviews with witnesses, field identification tests (showups), photoarrays, and lineups. See Table 6.1.

Two additional points about the Department of Justice guide are noteworthy. First, the guide describes good procedures for conducting simultaneous and sequential lineups, expresses no preference for one or the other presentation method. Second, the guide does not emphasize blind identification procedures over nonblind procedures. The panel members from the judicial system (and presumably their constituents) had not yet warmed to the idea

6
chapter

Table 6.1 | Key Points for Photoarrays and Lineups (Department of Justice, 1999)

- Instructions warning the witness that the perpetrator might not be in the array
- Minimum of five fillers
- Fillers selected on the basis of match to description
- Only one suspect in the array
- Consistent appearance of photos in the array
- Assess confidence prior to providing any feedback to the eyewitness
- Thoroughly document the identification procedure and outcome

of blind procedures (for more about the development of the guidelines, see Wells et al., 2000).

American Psychology-Law Society's White Paper on Best Practices in Identification Tests

In 1996 the American Psychology-Law Society's Executive Committee convened a committee to develop a set of recommended practices for lineups and photoarrays. These recommendations were published in *Law and Human Behavior* (Wells et al., 1998). This document not only provides the recommendations but also the rationale behind these recommendations and is a must-read for any expert witness proposing to offer expert testimony about system variables. The committee recommended four rules for identification tests (see Table 6.2).

International Association of the Chiefs of Police: Best Practices in Identification Tests

Finally, the International Association of the Chiefs of Police (IACP, 2006) also developed guidelines for best practices in collecting eyewitness identification evidence. The extent to which these recommendations are evidence-based is unclear as the document describing the guidelines does not provide a discussion of the process by which

Table 6.2 | Rules for Identification Tests (Wells et al., 1998)

- The person who conducts the lineup or photospread should not be aware of which member of the lineup or photospread is the suspect
- Eyewitnesses should be told explicitly that the person in question might not be in the lineup or photospread and therefore should not feel that they must make an identification. They should also be told that the person administering the lineup does not know which person is the suspect in the case
- The suspect should not stand out in the lineup or photospread as being different from the distractors based on the eyewitness's previous description of the culprit or based on other factors that would draw extra attention to the suspect
- A clear statement should be taken from the eyewitness at the time of the identification and prior to any feedback as to his confidence that the identified person is the actual culprit

these recommendations were created nor does the document itself refer to specific research on which the recommendations are based. With that in mind, the IACP has promulgated guidelines for both showups and lineups (live and photo), with an expressed preference for conducting lineups whenever possible. See Table 6.3 for some of IACP's recommendations for conducting showups.

These recommendations take into account research findings on some topics such as biased lineup instructions and confidence malleability but do not fully recognize other issues with showups such as clothing bias. Although the recommendations are against making the suspect don the perpetrator's clothing, it does not prohibit showing the suspect in clothing that matches the description of the perpetrator's clothing, which could increase the rate of mistaken identification if an innocent suspect just so happens to be wearing clothing that matches the clothing of the perpetrator.

The IACP recommends that similar instructions be given to witnesses viewing showups and lineups, with the additional

6
chapter

Table 6.3 | Recommendations for Conducting Showups (IACP, 2006)

- Showups should be used only when there is no other independent evidence to provide probable cause so that an arrest can be made
- The witness should provide a complete description of the perpetrator to the police before the showup is conducted
- The witness should be taken to the suspect rather than taking the suspect to the witness
- The witness should not view the suspect in a cell, in handcuffs, or in prison-issue clothing
- If there are multiple witnesses, showups should be conducted individually with each witness and the witnesses should not be allowed to communicate with each other about the procedure
- The suspect should never be presented more than once to the same witness
- Suspects should not be required to wear the perpetrator's clothing or imitate any of the perpetrator's actions or speech
- The showup administrator should not say anything to the witness suggesting that the suspect is the perpetrator, including any statements indicating that the suspect was found in the vicinity of the crime scene, that any evidence points to the suspect, or that other witnesses have identified the suspect
- Witnesses should provide statements about their confidence immediately after making an identification
- The witness should be instructed that (a) it is just as important to clear an innocent person of suspicion as it is to identify a guilty person, (b) the perpetrator may or may not be present, (c) the witness is not required to identify anyone, and (d) the investigation will continue irrespective of whether the witness identifies anyone

instruction that the appearance of the perpetrator may have changed during the intervening period between the commission of the crime and the identification procedure. In addition, and unlike the National Institute of Justice (NIJ) guidelines, the IACP recommends that the lineup be administered by an officer who does not know which lineup member is the suspect to prevent the transmission of any cues—intentional or unintentional—of the suspect's identity to the witness. The IACP also suggests that lineups be conducted sequentially rather than simultaneously and that lineups include five to six fillers who are chosen to look similar to other lineup members on dimensions such as race, gender, age, height, weight, hair color and style, facial hair, clothing, and other visible features such as eyeglasses or body art. Police officers are admonished to be careful to do nothing that would affect the reliability of the identification procedure, such as showing the witness photos of the suspect or conducting a showup prior to the lineup, and in the case of multiple witnesses, preventing the witnesses from speaking with one another. Finally, the IACP recommends that all lineups be videotaped to document the procedure used.

State Guidelines

Since the publication of the Department of Justice guide and the American Psychology-Law Society white paper, several states and jurisdictions have developed their own guidelines for identification procedures. Most notable are the states of New Jersey and North Carolina, which have adopted best practices state-wide. Their guidelines are very similar. They incorporate the best practices articulated in the Department of Justice guide, sequential presentation, and blind administration.

Limits of Comparison With Best Practices

Although comparing procedures used in a specific case with best practices is a fruitful approach, the exercise clearly has limitations. It is typical for the prosecutor to argue that the best practices do not apply to the specific jurisdiction. The Department of Justice guide is just that—a guide. The procedures endorsed in the guide are not required of local police departments. The NJ and NC guidelines certainly are not required in other states. Nevertheless, the exercise of comparing

BEWARE
Remember, best practices are guidelines rather than requirements.

procedures in a case to established best practices can be useful for demonstrating the science behind identification tests, giving legitimacy to the research, and educating the judge and jury about how faculty procedures could result in earnest but mistaken identification by highly confident witnesses.

Should Expert Testimony Be Offered in the Case?

After comprehensive review and interpretation of the data, experts should discuss their findings with the attorney so that the attorney can decide whether to offer expert testimony in the case. The attorney may request a report from the expert at this stage (see chapter 7 for suggestions for reports) or may prefer to discuss these matters without a report as the report may be discoverable in some jurisdictions.

Attorneys will want to know whether the expert testimony will help their case. The answer to this question will depend on the expert's findings concerning the levels and mix of general impairment factors, suspect bias factors, and postdictors. If, for example, there are general impairment factors (e.g., high stress, weapon focus, cross-race identification) and some suspect bias factors (e.g., nonblind lineup administrator, suggestive instructions, simultaneous presentation), the expert and attorney will probably conclude that expert testimony will be helpful in the case. If, in contrast, there are few general impairment and suspect bias factors, the attorney might choose not to offer the expert, for if the expert testifies, the testimony may benefit

INFO

When no suspect bias factors are present, expert testimony may be less useful to the defense.

the prosecutor's case more than the defendant's case. In our experience, prosecutors are rarely, if ever, interested in engaging eyewitness experts in an attempt to bolster the credibility of an eyewitness.

There is one less obvious scenario in which the usefulness of expert testimony is questionable, and that is when there are general impairment factors but no suspect bias factors. Consider, for example, a case involving cross-race recognition in which the witness was under considerable duress and had a gun pointed at him throughout the brief duration of the crime. Further suppose that the witness identified the suspect from a photoarray procedure that used best practices. An investigator who did not know which photo was the suspect's conducted the photoarray procedure. The instructions to the witness, given both orally and in writing, clearly conveyed that the perpetrator might not be present in the array and explained that it is very important not to implicate innocent suspects. The photoarray consisted of a suspect and photos of seven fillers matched to the description of the perpetrator. The investigator used the sequential presentation method. The expert testimony in this case might lead the jury to believe that the witness could not have gotten a good look at the perpetrator, but the photoarray test leaves little doubt that the positive identification was based on the witness's memory of the perpetrator, for the typical alternative explanations for the positive identification— guessing, deduction, and investigator influence—are for the most part ruled out through the use of best practices. In this situation, testimony about general impairment factors is unlikely to be helpful to the jury, and if she takes the stand, the expert is likely to be cross-examined about the identification procedures, which appeared very good. In conclusion, expert testimony is most likely to be helpful in cases in which there are suspect bias factors.

Report Writing and Testimony | 7

E xperts communicate their findings in several ways. First, after reviewing discovery and forming opinions, the expert reports these opinions to the attorney orally, in writing, or both orally and in writing. Second, assuming the case goes forward and the attorney chooses to proffer the expert testimony, experts communicate their findings in court. Prior to testifying to the jury, however, experts may have to first testify in an admissibility hearing so that the judge can determine whether the expert testimony will be admitted in court.

Reporting Expert Opinions

The expert's report can take one of several forms. Some attorneys request an affidavit. Others do not require a specific format and will even accept an e-mailed summary of the expert's findings. Regardless of the format, we recommend that the report include the elements listed in Table 7.1.

The description of the expert's credentials should be brief. The attorney should have a copy of the expert's CV and submit it with the report and as an exhibit at an admissibility hearing or at a trial if the expert's testimony is admitted. The description of the discovery materials reviewed should be specific—the attorneys should be able to identify the specific document reviewed by its description in the report. The overview of the research on mistaken identification and erroneous conviction generally makes the point that mistaken identification is one of the leading precursors of erroneous conviction and helps support the need for expert testimony. The summary of

Table 7.1 | Recommended Report Elements

1. A brief description of the expert's credentials
2. A brief description of the expert's experience as a consultant and expert witness in eyewitness cases
3. A brief description of how the expert became involved in the case and discovery materials reviewed
4. An overview of research on mistaken identification and erroneous conviction
5. A summary of the research about each case-relevant factor affecting the accuracy of eyewitness identifications
6. A summary of the research addressing the consensus of experts regarding the reliability of case-relevant factors that influence identification accuracy
7. A summary of research testing whether knowledge about eyewitness factors is a matter of commonsense

each relevant factor serves as a preview of the expert testimony. In this section, the attorneys and the judges learn the substance of the expert testimony. It is important to emphasize that the opinions are based on published research, so citations and full references should be included.

We recommend that the expert also summarize the research on general consensus and common sense (see chapter 3). Our recommendation is based on the fact that prosecutors frequently challenge the admissibility of expert testimony by claiming that there is no general consensus about the research or that the research does not go beyond the common sense of the jury. Testifying about the research that demonstrates consensus and demonstrates that the research findings are sometimes at odds with common sense helps the defense attorney overcome these admissibility challenges. Further, the report provides the first opportunity to

BEST PRACTICE

Support opinions and the need for expert testimony with appropriate documentation such as citations to published research.

inform the judge that there is a corpus of empirical research addressing consensus among experts and common sense about eyewitness research.

Preparing for Expert Testimony

Many attorneys are inexperienced with respect to eyewitness experts. An experienced expert may have much more experience testifying as an expert than the attorney has retaining and working with experts. The expert, therefore, should be in a good position to educate the attorney about the preferred ebb and flow of expert testimony.

Providing Sample Questions

We recommend that the expert offer to provide the attorney with a list of sample questions for establishing the expert's qualifications—referred to by some attorneys as voir dire of the expert—and for direct testimony. These questions should pertain to the expert's qualifications and should be designed to elicit testimony about the relevant factors in the case (see below for more detail about the questions). In our experience, the attorney always eagerly accepts this offer for the attorney benefits in two ways. First, the attorney learns from the experiences of the expert, and, second, the gesture saves the attorney a good deal of work. Note that we used the phrase "sample questions." The direct examination is the responsibility of the attorney. He may give the sample questions careful consideration and ultimately may use some or all of them, but the decision is that of the attorney, not that of the expert.

Pretrial Conference

Prior to the trial, we recommend that the expert and the attorney confer for an hour or two about expert testimony. The attorney will often require such a conference. This conference can take place by telephone, at a meeting the night before trial, or during an extended trial break. The expert and the attorney should attempt to fulfill several objectives with this conference.

BEST PRACTICE

Provide the attorney with a list of sample questions to consider for direct examination.

7
chapter

The expert should approach this conference with the following perspectives: the attorney is in charge of the questions, and the expert is in charge of the answers. The expert can recommend questions to the attorney, but the attorney must ultimately decide which questions to ask and how to ask them. Attorneys may provide guidance to experts about how to answer questions, but the answers must by the expert's, not the attorney's.

REVIEWING QUESTIONS FOR DIRECT EXAMINATION

One objective of the conference is to review the planned questions for direct examination together. Reviewing the questions has several benefits. Some attorneys will want to preview the expert's answers and take the opportunity to advise the expert about the use of certain language, identify aspects of the expert's testimony that are unclear, and recommend topics that deserve further elaboration. Reviewing all of the planned questions gives experts an opportunity to make sure that attorneys understand the expected answers to the questions they have written. This is an important step because many attorneys do not have a command over the eyewitness research and may have some unrealistic expectations about the expert's testimony. The attorney, for example, may believe that an eyewitness who gives inconsistent descriptions of a perpetrator is unlikely to be capable of correctly identifying the suspect from a photoarray; however, as noted in chapter 3, research does not support this claim. An attorney with this set of case facts and beliefs may plan to ask the expert about the relation between consistency of descriptions and identification accuracy. The expert should inform the attorney during conference of the answer and give the attorney the opportunity to rethink the question. Of course, the attorney will make the final decision about whether to ask the question but it is the expert's duty to make sure the attorney knows the answer that the question will receive; the expert's answer should not change to support the position of the attorney if research does not support the attorney's construal of the facts.

BEWARE
Attorneys may have unrealistic expectations about expert testimony. These can be corrected during a pretrial conference.

PREPARING FOR CROSS-EXAMINATION

A second objective of the attorney–expert pretrial conference is to review the likely substance of cross-examination. In the following sections we review some of the approaches to cross-examination in admissibility hearings and at trial. The pretrial conference can be used, therefore, to blunt some of the issues expected on cross-examination and also to plan redirect examination. With respect to the former, some attorneys attempt to steal the opponent's thunder. They attempt this by raising issues during direct examination that are expected to be raised by the opposing attorney during cross-examination. The message conveyed using this approach is that the expert is aware of the limitations raised by the opposing attorney but does not think that these limitations outweigh the main message delivered on direct examination. For example, if the defense attorney expects the prosecuting attorney to challenge the admissibility of expert testimony based in part on the fact that most of the eyewitness research uses crime simulation methods, the defense attorney might choose to establish this fact during direct examination. Doing so enables the attorney to question the expert about why crime simulation methods are used, why it is important to the science, and why the benefits of crime simulation methods outweigh the drawbacks. It also limits the "surprise" factor. When this point is raised during cross-examination, the jury will already be aware of it.

The strategy of raising such limitations during direct examination, however, is risky. The defense attorney who uses this strategy may end up raising weaknesses that may never have been raised by the prosecuting attorney because the defense attorney does not actually know what the prosecuting attorney is intending to ask during cross-examination. For this reason, some attorneys do not use this strategy and instead plan to address issues if raised in cross-examination during redirect examination. The pretrial conference is the

BEST PRACTICE

Use the pretrial conference to

● review the questions for direct examination
● prepare for cross-examination
● learn about the particular court culture and players
● review courtroom etiquette

7
chapter

ideal opportunity to put all of these issues on the table and to give the attorney the opportunity to decide how to handle them.

SOCIALIZING THE EXPERT

The pretrial conference gives the attorney the opportunity to socialize the expert about the particular court culture, prosecuting attorney, judge, and jury. Prosecuting attorneys differ in the levels of intelligence, preparedness, aggressiveness, deference, and investment in the particular case. The same prosecuting attorney may be more prepared for or more invested in one case than in another. The judge may be keenly interested in hearing an eyewitness expert (a relatively new and unique form of testimony), hostile toward this form of testimony, indifferent, or disengaged. Some judges are inclined to ask questions of the experts. Some judges grant the expert considerable leeway in answering open-ended questions, whereas others keep experts on a tight leash. Juries may vary with respect to the levels of education and professional orientations of their members and to their open-mindedness toward experts from outside their communities. Experienced attorneys will have insights regarding the characteristics of the prosecuting attorney, judge, and jury and should convey their thoughts to their experts. From the experts' perspective, it is always helpful to know something about the people with whom they are about to interact for the first time.

REVIEW OF COURTROOM ETIQUETTE

Last, the attorney may use the pretrial conference to remind the expert of courtroom etiquette issues. The attorney may advise the expert to face the jury when answering questions, to speak loudly and clearly, and to use plain language and simple sentences. Attorneys typically do not want their experts to appear overly defensive during cross-examination or to argue with the opposing attorney or judge.

Direct and Cross-Examination During Admissibility Hearings

The purpose of the admissibility hearing is for the judge to decide whether the proffered expert testimony will be admitted at trial. The hearing provides the attorneys with the opportunity to present arguments in favor of or against expert testimony. The attorneys may also be given the opportunity to submit their arguments in writing. As part of the hearing, the court may preview the proposed expert testimony. In these cases, the attorneys and expert must prepare for the direct examination and cross-examination as they would in anticipation of a jury trial.

Differences From a Jury Trial

There are some important differences in the examination and cross-examination of the expert in the admissibility hearing as compared to the jury trial. First, the goal is different. As explained above, the purpose of the admissibility hearing is to give the judge the information necessary to decide whether the expert testimony should be admitted. In contrast, the purpose of the jury trial is to give the jury enough information to decide whether the prosecution has proven the defendant's guilt beyond a reasonable doubt. Second, because of the different goals of these two proceedings, the questions asked of the expert may be somewhat different in the two types of proceedings. Third, there is no jury present during an admissibility hearing; consequently, the expert does not speak to the jury but rather to the attorneys and the judge. Differences in audiences mean differences in deportment and language.

Challenges to Admissibility

The admissibility hearing addresses the science behind expert testimony. As explained in chapter 1, the federal courts use the *Daubert* standard (*Daubert v. Merrell Dow Pharmaceuticals*, 1993), the gist of which is that the science on which the proposed expert testimony is based is reliable and valid. Some states have adopted some version of the *Daubert* standard. Other states continue to use the *Frye* standard (*Frye v. United States*, 1923), which requires that the science be generally accepted in the scientific community. In addition, the Federal Rules of Evidence (1975) require that the expert testimony be helpful to the jury and that its probative value outweigh its prejudicial impact.

Opponents of expert testimony may challenge its admissibility from each of these perspectives. Using the Federal Rules of Evidence, the opposing attorney may argue that the expert's testimony is merely a matter of common sense, and jurors possess the requisite knowledge to evaluate eyewitness memory (cf, Schmechel et al., 2006). They may further argue that the expert testimony will prejudice the jury—that it will generally create an unnecessary and unwarranted doubt in eyewitness testimony, causing jurors to discredit even reliable eyewitness testimony. The Federal Rules of Evidence also specify the qualifications required of experts. The opposing attorney may argue that the person should not be considered an expert under the courts' rules and therefore should not be permitted to testify. Alternatively, the opposing attorney may argue that the eyewitness research upon which the expert testimony is based is not generally accepted in the scientific community and therefore does not meet the *Frye* standard. Although the *Daubert* standard superseded the *Frye* standard in the federal courts and in some states, general acceptance is still a factor given consideration under the *Daubert* standard. With the *Daubert* standard in mind, the opposing attorney might argue that the scientific foundation of the expert testimony is unreliable—that it is junk science.

Designing the Direct Examination

A carefully designed direct examination will provide a compelling demonstration of the usefulness of the testimony while addressing the five challenges described above and summarized in the following questions:

1. Is the person qualified to testify as an expert witness?
2. Is the content of the expert testimony within the ken of the jury?
3. Does the expert testimony's probative value outweigh its prejudicial impact?
4. Is scientific research generally accepted in the field?
5. Is the expert testimony based on "junk science"?

In the following we illustrate how these objectives can be met through the development of a line of questioning. We divide the direct examination into four sections.

VOIR DIRE

The first section is the voir dire of the expert—the procedure used to establish the person's qualifications to testify as an expert witness.

Voir dire is the first part of the direct examination and is conducted by the defense attorney—the attorney who proffered the expert—but the opposing attorney and judge have the opportunity to ask questions as well once the defense attorney has asked all of his questions. Voir dire can begin with some general questions concerning the expert's identity and how she became involved in the case (see Table 7.2).

Table 7.2 | Examples of Questions for Voir Dire

- Would you please state your name for the jury?
- What is your address?
- What is your occupation?
- How did you get involved in this case?
- What materials have you reviewed in this case?
- Did you formulate any opinions regarding this case?
- Were you later retained by the defense to offer those opinions at this trial?
- Before we discuss your opinions about this case, could you briefly tell the jury about your educational training?
- Did you specialize in any particular field within psychology?
- Would you please give the jury a brief description of your employment since receiving your doctorate?
- Please tell the jury the sort of classes that you teach or have taught?
- Are you a member of any professional associations?
- Do you hold an office with any of these professional associations?
- I am showing you what's been marked as Ex. __ (CV). Have you seen this document before?
- Would you tell the court what this document is?
- Have you ever conducted research in the field of human memory and eyewitness identification?
- Have you ever received grants for your research on eyewitness memory?
- Have you written books or book chapters on the topic of eyewitness memory?

7
chapter

- Turning back to your resume, you list several pages of "refereed journal articles." What is a "refereed journal"?
- About how many papers on eyewitness memory have you published in refereed journals?
- What were the names of some of these journals?
- Have you ever been asked to give speeches at professional conferences?
- Do you teach about the topic of eyewitness memory in your university classes?
- Have you ever received any awards or honors for your work?
- Are you a member of any professional organizations?
- Have you ever held an office in any professional organization?
- Have you ever testified at a criminal trial before?
- Have you served as an advisor to any police departments or courts about the psychology of eyewitness memory?
- Do you continue to do research in the field of eyewitness memory and identification?

Answers to the above questions should permit the judge to make a determination about the expert's qualifications to testify at trial.

SCIENTIFIC RESEARCH

The second section of the direct examination would focus on the science of eyewitness testimony. Its purpose is to convey the depth of science on eyewitness memory and related topics and address several of the challenges—whether the expert testimony is within the ken of the jury and the general acceptance and quality of the scientific research (see Table 7.3).

RELEVANT FACTORS

The third section addresses the specific general impairment factors, suspect bias factors, and postdictors identified by the expert as relevant in this case. Some experts prefer to preface this section with a general testimony about the stages of memory (encoding,

Table 7.3 | Examples of Questions for Scientific Research

- Do psychologists conduct scientific research on human memory?
- On what basis do you call the research on human memory scientific?
- Have there been scientific publications on human memory?
- Can you in some way quantify the amount of scientific research on human memory?
- For how long have psychologists been conducting scientific experiments on eyewitness memory?
- Can you quantify the amount of scientific research on eyewitness memory?
- Can you explain how research on eyewitness identification is conducted, perhaps by giving an example of an eyewitness identification experiment?
- Has this research been subject to peer review?
- Are there published summaries of eyewitness memory research?
- Are there meta-analyses of eyewitness memory research?
- Would you explain what is meant by the term "meta-analysis"?
- Are meta-analyses subjected to peer review?
- Has this research led to some general conclusions about eyewitness identification?
- Can you give some examples of these conclusions?

storage retrieval), the reconstructive nature of memory, and counter myths such as the erroneous belief that memory works like a video recorder. Such general testimony can be given in response to a very general question, such as "does memory work like a video recorder?" with a prompt for explanation and can flow naturally into questions about specific factors. For each factor, the attorney should ask—and the expert should answer—a series of questions designed to accomplish the following:

1. define the factor,
2. give an example of a study examining that factor,

7
chapter

3. establish that the studies have been subjected to peer review,
4. describe general conclusions from the literature concerning the factor's relationship to identification accuracy, and
5. the general acceptance of the factor within the scientific community.

These questions can be prefaced with some general questions about the factors, such as the first two questions in Table 7.4. The following set of questions can then be repeated for each factor identified by the expert. Some of the questions, for example, those asking the expert to describe the research on general acceptance and common sense and to indicate whether that research has been subjected to peer review, may not need to be repeated for each factor, but the research findings concerning general acceptance and common sense should be repeated.

Table 7.4 | Examples of Questions on Relevant Factors

- In your review of the information in this case, were you able to identify factors that may have impaired the eyewitness's memories for the perpetrator?
- What factors did you identify?
- Let's talk about each of those separately if we could. What is meant by the term cross-race recognition?
- Can you give an example of a scientific study of the effect of cross-race recognition?
- Have there been any meta-analyses of the effects of cross-race identification on the accuracy of eyewitness identifications?
- What do those meta-analyses show?
- Have studies of cross-race recognition been published in peer-reviewed journals?
- What do you conclude based on this research?
- Is this conclusion generally accepted among scientists who conduct research on eyewitness memory?

(Continued)

- How do you know that this conclusion or any conclusion from the research is generally accepted?
- Have there been scientific studies of general acceptance of eyewitness research?
- Can you describe these studies?
- Has this research been subjected to peer review?
- Is the cross-race effect, in your opinion, a matter of common sense?
- Have there been scientific studies of whether the cross-race effect is a matter of common sense?
- Would you describe these studies?
- Has this research been subjected to peer review?

COMPARISON WITH BEST PRACTICES

The fourth set of questions pertains to the comparison of the identification procedures with "best practices." This section has several purposes. First, at trial, it will provide the judge and jury with some benchmarks against which the identification procedure used in the case can be compared. Second, the adoption of best practices by the Department of Justice, several states, and other police departments can be used as arguments that the research foundation is reliable and that it is generally accepted not only in the scientific community but in law enforcement communities (see Table 7.5).

Cross-Examination and Redirect

It is important to anticipate possible cross-examination strategies on each set of issues. An expert who has been through these hearings a few times may find that the cross-examination questions become predictable—the more so given that attorneys share strategies with one another. Using the sample direct examination sequence above, we will review possible cross-examination strategies by section and discuss how these items can be addressed during redirect examination.

Table 7.5 | Examples of Questions for Comparison with Best Practices

- Has the research on photoarray procedures led to published recommendations or "best practices"?
- Where have those recommendations been published?
- Have they been subjected to peer review?
- Have these recommendations been adopted in other states or police departments?
- Why have these recommendations been adopted by other states? Why have they sought to change their identification procedures?

VOIR DIRE

The first section was the voir dire, intended to establish the person's qualifications to testify as an expert witness. One obvious line of cross-examination pertains to weak credentials. The surveys published by Kassin et al. (1989, 2001) identify the typical qualifications of experts who completed surveys. Their expertise, as measured by publications records, is substantial. A person with a weak record or no record of scholarship on eyewitness memory runs the risk of being disqualified as an expert. Among experts with strong research records, prosecutors may question the expert about his role in research on individual factors about which he proposes to testify. One expert, for example, may have studied suggestive identification procedures for 25 years and may have published numerous comprehensive reviews of the eyewitness literature in books and book chapters but may never have conducted empirical research on cross-race recognition. A prosecutor may argue that this expert is qualified to discuss research on suggestive identification procedures but not cross-race recognition, and the judge may accept this argument. The judge is not obligated to allow expert testimony on an all-or-none basis; rather, the judge may choose to admit expert testimony about some topics but not others. Another approach is to question the expert's experience with actual police procedures. The experience of many eyewitness experts is limited to research and expert testimony. Many eyewitness experts have never consulted with police departments about their procedures. A prosecutor may argue that the expert's lack of experience with police work disqualifies her to testify about police procedures.

Weaknesses in the expert's publication record can be addressed on redirect by emphasizing the knowledge and experience of the expert through other sources, such as the teaching of knowledge about eyewitness memory in university courses. The expert may have a respectable publication record in related topics, such as human memory or social influence. Redirect can be used to establish the relevance of expertise in these areas to eyewitness research. According to the Federal Rules of Evidence, simply stated, an expert is someone who knows more than the jury. The rules do not require that the expert have a publication record on a given topic or at all. When the prosecutor questions an expert's empirical research history on a given topic, for example, cross-race recognition, redirect can focus on the expert's record of writing about cross-race recognition in scholarly publications such as books and book chapters. Doing so should encourage the judge to conclude that the expert knows more than the jury about cross-race recognition. When the prosecutor exposes the expert's lack of experience working with police personnel, redirect can be used to establish that research about which the expert will testify (e.g., suggestive identification procedures) has been embraced by some police departments and formulated into best practices.

INFO

Immediately following cross-examination, the defense is given the opportunity for redirect examination (typically abbreviated as "redirect"). The scope of a redirect is limited to issues raised during cross-examination. Immediately following a redirect, the prosecuting attorney is given the opportunity for a "recross," that is, to ask additional questions about topics covered during the redirect. Judges may interject questions at any time in the proceeding.

SCIENTIFIC RESEARCH

The second section of direct examination focused on the scientific foundation underlying the expert's testimony. Here the cross-examination is likely to focus on the research methodology. The prosecutor will want to establish that the vast majority of research on eyewitness identification uses crime simulation methods rather than actual crimes, that most of the research uses university students (as opposed to a more representative sample of citizens likely to be exposed to crime), that the simulations are relative innocuous events, and that identification decisions have no real consequences for the witnesses or the perpetrators. The prosecutor might also raise the fact that some vocal psychologists have challenged the generalizability of the eyewitness research to actual cases at conferences, in print, and in court. These are valid points, and they should be acknowledged. Some of these points may have already been raised during direct examination. During redirect examination, the expert can reiterate the benefits of crime simulation research and use of college students as witnesses, as summarized in chapter 3. The expert can indicate that not all of the research is crime simulation research—there is a growing trend toward field studies. The expert can point out that not all witnesses are victims of dangerous crimes; some are asked to identify suspects who were witnessed under innocuous circumstances (e.g., in the vicinity before a crime). Another point in support of the generalizability of the eyewitness research is that the products of the research, such as improvements to identification tests, have been adopted in practice by a growing number of police departments.

RELEVANT FACTORS

The third section of direct examination focused on the specific eyewitness factors relevant to the case. This section provides plenty of fodder for cross-examination. The prosecutor might challenge the expert's general conclusion from the research, perhaps by asking the expert about specific studies whose results do not support the general conclusion. Alternatively, the prosecutor might ask about factors that could qualify the general conclusion and the status of research on these potential qualifying factors. As examples of these points, it would

BEST PRACTICE

Acknowledge the limitations of scientific research and address them accordingly during redirect.

not be difficult for a prosecutor to find a study of cross-race recognition that does not show the typical cross-race recognition effect, as the magnitude of the main effects for race of witness and perpetrator vary among the studies. There are some studies that do not find the cross-race effect, at least under some circumstances. With respect to qualifying conditions, the prosecutor might ask about the relevant role of experience with members of the other race. Has the research examined whether the cross-race effect occurs among White citizens who have lived in predominantly Black communities for 30 years? Most of the studies have used witnesses who at the time of the study were younger than 30. Most of the research on cross-race recognition examines White and Black witnesses and perpetrators, though some have included Hispanic or Asian individuals (e.g., Platz & Hosch, 1988). Many cities in the United States have become culturally diverse and so the combinations of witness and perpetrator race have expanded considerably, especially when one considers that there is considerable within-group heterogeneity of appearance. A prosecutor might question whether the existing research on the cross-race effect generalizes to a case in which a store owner, an immigrant from Pakistan, reports having been robbed by a perpetrator who appeared to be of Puerto Rican origin. The expert must acknowledge that some research findings are at odds with general conclusions, as in any area of science, but that meta-analysis shows that the trends are supported by the data. The expert must acknowledge that we do not have a full understanding of the factors that may qualify the general conclusion. In some cases, we have only modest understanding about the qualifying factors (see, e.g., McQuiston-Surrett, Malpass, & Tredoux, 2006).

Another theme of cross-examination focuses on general acceptance. The expert may have offered an opinion that the conclusion about a specific factor is generally accepted in the scientific community and may have discussed the Kassin et al. (2001) survey in support of that opinion. The Kassin et al. study, however, has been subjected to rigorous cross-examination. Prosecutors have pointed out through questioning of the expert that the sample is selective

BEWARE
Our general conclusions about the factors that influence identification accuracy are limited by our understanding of their qualifying conditions.

7
chapter

(i.e., not every psychologist who studies memory responded or was even sampled), that the number of experts in the "high" consensus sample is not large, that some of the findings (e.g., effects of stress) do not meet with high levels of consensus, that it is not clear who the experts in the study are (it was anonymous, of course), and that it is not known whether psychologists known to disagree with the findings were surveyed. On redirect examination, the expert can note that the Kassin et al. studies were published in one of psychology's most prestigious scientific journals (*American Psychologist*) and that the survey methodology was in keeping with rigorous expectations for research. The expert can also point out that the Kassin et al. studies are just one source of information about general acceptance. The general conclusions from eyewitness research are echoed in numerous scientific articles, scholarly books, book chapters, conference presentations, textbooks and in university course lectures through the United States and Europe.

Yet another line of cross-examination pertains to the extent of knowledge about the specific factor. Consider, for example, the effect of stress on identification accuracy. Experts typically testify that extreme stress impairs identification accuracy. The prosecutor may ask the expert *how much* stress impairs identification accuracy. With respect to retention interval, the prosecutor might ask what the research has to say about the decrease in accuracy one might expect with a retention interval of 7 days. How much exposure time is needed for an accurate identification? What does research say about the effect of stress on *this witness's* memory? These are good questions, but research does not provide the answers. The expert must acknowledge that research has limitations.

Last, the prosecutor can be expected to argue that the research findings—even if deemed reliable—are within the ken of the jury and the expert testimony is therefore not needed. The prosecutor may identify some factors as particularly commonsensical and ask the expert about them. Wouldn't the average person know that the longer time you have to view a perpetrator, the more likely you are to correctly identify him? Wouldn't the average person know that

BEWARE
Eyewitness research does not permit conclusions about the accuracy of individual eyewitnesses in specific cases.

identifications made after a long period of time are less likely to be accurate than identifications made immediately after the crime? These factors are a matter of common sense (see Kassin et al., 2001). Other factors, such as cross-race recognition and stress, are not a matter of common sense, as reviewed in chapter 3. Nevertheless, the prosecutors have the *hindsight bias* working in their favor. Once you learn something new, it seems like you have known it all along. So convincing judges that something they have just learned is not a matter of common sense may be difficult.

BEWARE Both the prosecutor and judge may fall prey to the hindsight bias and conclude that the information provided by the expert is something they knew without benefit of the expert's testimony.

All of the research on common sense may be placed under the microscope. Surveys of lay knowledge may be picked apart item by item, and these surveys are far from perfect. Trial simulations in which mock juror's decisions in eyewitness cases are evaluated may be subjected to the same criticisms as crime simulation research. The trial simulations may lack some important elements of real trials (e.g., rigorous cross-examination, judges' instructions on the relevant law), the participants are often university students and not representative of jury pools, and there are no real consequences of the mock jurors' decisions. On redirect examination, the expert can note that although none of the studies on lay knowledge are perfect and that the various methodologies have different strengths and weaknesses, yet a large body of this research converges on the conclusion that some of these factors are not a matter of common sense. The expert can also note that the lineup reform movement supports the view that many factors affecting identification decisions are not a matter of common sense. Police departments have been doing lineups for many years. These reforms would have been implemented years ago if they were merely a matter of common sense.

COMPARISON WITH BEST PRACTICES

The fourth section of direct examination involved comparison of identification procedures used in the case to established "best practices." The prosecutor may cross-examine the expert on the relevance of the best-practice documents for the particular

BEWARE
Prosecutors may challenge best practices as not legally binding and may expose the inconsistencies in recommendations among the sets of best practices.

jurisdiction. Depending upon which "best practices" the expert relies (see previous section for examples of sets of best practices, such as the Department of Justice recommendations or the IACP recommendations), the best practices would entail some combination of instructions warning the witness that the perpetrator might not be present in the lineup, selection of fillers that match the perpetrator's description, sequential presentation, and blind administration (these are the practices adopted in New Jersey, North Carolina, and elsewhere). The Department of Justice guidelines, however, are guidelines, not policy. The fact that New Jersey and North Carolina have changed their procedures has no legal bearing on other states, and prosecutors may use the opportunity to emphasize the independence and priorities of their districts.

A prosecutor might use cross-examination on this topic to note that there are inconsistencies among the best-practice documents. For example, the Department of Justice guidelines describe simultaneous and sequential presentation but do not advocate the use of one procedure over the other. The New Jersey and North Carolina procedures, by contrast, require the use of double-blind sequential lineups. As another compelling example, the Department of Justice guidelines do not recommend the use of double-blind lineups, whereas the New Jersey and North Carolina procedures require it. On redirect, the expert can clarify that best practices evolve over time, and it is not uncommon for better practices to supersede previous best practices. Within a given time period, there is less inconsistency among best practices on eyewitness identification.

Direct and Cross-Examination During the Trial

Much of the direct and cross-examination that occurred during the admissibility hearing can be replicated at trial, although there are some important differences.

Audience

One difference is that the judge is the audience in an admissibility hearing, whereas the jury is the audience at a trial. (The expert should remain mindful that creating a record for appeal is typically one of the attorney's goals for both hearings.) With the jury as the audience, the expert should

BEST PRACTICE

When testifying before a jury, adapt your style and level of research detail to maximize comprehension by the jury.

make extra efforts to use plain-language explanations, to elaborate on complex issues, to give concrete examples, to be a little repetitive, and to be a little animated so as to keep the jury's attention, as research shows that experts who are concrete and repetitive in their explanations are more influential (Kovera, Gresham, Borgida, Gray, & Regan, 1997). Put another way, testifying to a jury as an expert witness is somewhat like lecturing to undergraduate students, and some of the techniques that lead to effective teaching also lead to effective expert testimony.

Substance

Besides style, there are some differences in the substance of expert testimony between an admissibility hearing and a testimony before the jury. For example, having heard the qualifications of the expert during the admissibility hearing, the prosecutor may choose to stipulate to the expert's expertise and waive the voir dire questioning. This is a strategic decision in which the prosecuting attorney does not want the jury to hear a lot about the expert's qualifications. When this happens, the defense attorney is normally allowed to ask a few questions about the expert's qualifications to establish the context for the testimony to follow.

Level of Research Detail

One of the main areas of difference is the level of detail in describing the research. Defense attorneys differ widely in the level of research detail they desire. At one extreme, some defense attorneys will want the jury to hear all of the detail that was raised on the admissibility hearing. At another extreme, some defense attorneys will want to omit all of the detail about the research and have the experts merely summarize the conclusions of the research. For example, following the voir dire section, the defense attorney may entirely omit the above section on the science underlying the research and proceed as follows:

- In your review of the information in this case, were you able to identify factors that may have impaired the eyewitness's memories for the perpetrator?
- What factors did you identify?
- Let's talk about each of those separately if we could. What is meant by the term cross-race recognition?
- What do you conclude based on this research?

The last two questions are then repeated for each of the relevant factors. Thus, there may be no discussion about the volume of eyewitness research, the research methodology, the strengths and weaknesses of crime simulations, the sample studies of relevant factors, or consensus among experts. In this version, experts merely give their opinions about the conclusions based on the research. Of course, the level of detail can be somewhere between the two extremes. The expert may express preferences for one approach over another, but ultimately the decision regarding which questions to ask is the responsibility of the defense attorney. It should be noted that just because the defense attorney omits questions about the research methodology, it does not preclude the prosecutor from cross-examining on these issues.

Specific Issues

Some of the issues raised during admissibility hearings are specific for the admissibility hearings, such as whether the testimony is within the common understanding of the jury. The issue of whether eyewitness research is within the ken of the jury is relevant to arguments in favor or opposed to expert testimony and does not address the issue that the jury must decide.

BEWARE
The prosecutor may question research methodology even if the defense does not address it during direct testimony.

Assessing Expert Testimony

Psychologists who desire to practice expert testimony regularly should have an interest in improving their skills. We recommend that experts seek and obtain feedback from the attorneys with whom they have worked. Sometime after the conclusion of the trial, the expert should set up a time to speak with the attorney by telephone. The purpose of the phone call is to request constructive feedback on one's performance as an expert witness. Attorneys are normally candid and appreciate being asked. The attorney might provide the expert with practical advice, such as make more eye contact with the jury, use more parochial language, and do not be so defensive—if there are limitations to the research, just acknowledge them. The attorney may simply say that it was a job well done, and this is always reinforcing to hear. The expert will undoubtedly learn about the trial outcome but should not take it as evidence of his skills. Trial outcomes are multiply determined. Further, there are some cases in which the defense attorney has little or no expectation of winning because the evidence is overwhelming, the prosecution has not offered an attractive plea, or the defendant insists on going to trial.

Conclusion

Providing expert testimony about the reliability of eyewitness identification evidence can be an important service. Jurors appear unaware of many of the factors that influence the accuracy of eyewitness identifications and expert testimony on the relevant research may help the jurors gauge the appropriate weight to give to an identification gained under a particular set of circumstances. Moreover, it is possible that jurisdictions will be moved to reform their identification procedures if they are frequently contested in court. To be effective, however, eyewitness experts need to be well versed in the current research on eyewitness reliability and to recognize the limitations of the research and the expertise that they provide.

7
chapter

References

Behrman, B. W., & Davey, S. L. (2001). Eyewitness identification in actual criminal cases: An archival analysis. *Law and Human Behavior, 25,* 475–491.

Behrman, B. W., & Richards, R. E. (2005). Suspect/foil identification in actual crimes and in the laboratory: A reality monitoring analysis. *Law and Human Behavior, 29,* 279–301.

Borchard, E. M. (1932). *Convicting the innocent.* Garden City, NY: Garden City Publishing Company.

Bradfield, A. L., Wells, G. L., & Olson, E. A. (2002). The damaging effect of confirming feedback on the relation between eyewitness certainty and identification accuracy. *Journal of Applied Psychology, 87,* 112–120.

Brigham, J. C., Maass, A., Snyder, L. D., & Spaulding, K. (1982). Accuracy of eyewitness identifications in a field setting. *Journal of Personality and Social Psychology, 42,* 673–681.

Brigham, J. C., Meissner, C. A., & Wasserman, A. W. (1999). Applied issues in the construction and expert assessment of photo lineups. *Applied Cognitive Psychology, 13,* S73–S92.

Buckhout, R., Rabinowitz, M., Alfonso, V., Kanellis, D., & Anderson, J. (1988). Empirical assessment of lineups: Getting down to cases. *Law and Human Behavior, 12,* 323–331.

Clark, S. E. (2005). A re-examination of the effects of biased lineup instructions in eyewitness identification. *Law and Human Behavior, 29,* 395–424.

Clark, S. E., & Tunnicliff, J. L. (2001). Selecting lineup foils in eyewitness identification experiments: Experimental control and real-world simulation. *Law and Human Behavior, 25,* 199–216.

Clifford, B. R., & Scott, J. (1978). Individual and situational factors in eyewitness testimony. *Journal of Applied Psychology, 63,* 352–359.

Copple, R. W., Torkildson J., & Kovera, M. B. (2008). Expert psychological testimony: Admissibility standards. In B. L. Cutler (Ed.), *Encyclopedia of psychology and law* (pp. 271–275). Thousand Oaks, CA: Sage Publications.

Cutler, B. L. (2006). A sample of witness, crime, and perpetrator characteristics affecting eyewitness identification accuracy. *Cardozo Public Law, Policy, and Ethics Journal, 4,* 327–340.

Cutler, B. L., Dexter, H. R., & Penrod, S. D. (1989). Expert testimony and jury decision making: An empirical analysis. *Behavioral Sciences and the Law, 7,* 215–225.

Cutler, B. L., & Penrod, S. D. (1988). Improving the reliability of eyewitness identification: Lineup construction and presentation. *Journal of Applied Psychology, 73*, 281–290.

Cutler, B. L., & Penrod, S. D. (1995). *Mistaken identification: The eyewitness, psychology, & the law.* Cambridge: Cambridge University Press.

Cutler, B. L., Penrod, S. D., & Dexter, H. R. (1989). The eyewitness, the expert psychologist, and the jury. *Law and Human Behavior, 13*, 311–332.

Cutler, B. L., Penrod, S. D., & Dexter, H. R. (1990). Juror sensitivity to eyewitness identification evidence. *Law and Human Behavior, 14*, 185–191.

Cutler, B. L., Penrod, S. D., & Martens, T. K. (1987a). The reliability of eyewitness identification: The role of system and estimator variables. *Law and Human Behavior, 11*, 223–238.

Cutler, B. L., Penrod, S. D., & Martens, T. K. (1987b). Improving the reliability of eyewitness identification: Putting context into context. *Journal of Applied Psychology, 72*, 629–637.

Cutler, B. L., Penrod, S. D., O'Rourke, T. E., & Martens, T. K. (1986). Unconfounding the effects of contextual cues on eyewitness identification accuracy. *Social Behaviour, 1*, 113–134.

Deffenbacher, K. A. (1980). Eyewitnesses accuracy and confidence: Can we infer anything about their relationship? *Law and Human Behavior, 4*, 243–260.

Deffenbacher, K. A., Bornstein, B. H., & Penrod, S. D. (2006). Mugshot exposure effects: Retroactive interference, mugshot commitment, source confusion, and unconscious transference. *Law and Human Behavior, 30*, 287–307.

Deffenbacher, K. A., Bornstein, B. H., Penrod, S. D., & McGorty, E. K. (2004). A meta-analytic review of the effects of high stress on eyewitness memory. *Law and Human Behavior, 28*, 687–706.

Devenport, J. L., & Cutler, B. L. (2004). Impact of defense-only and opposing eyewitness experts on juror judgments. *Law and Human Behavior, 28*, 569–576.

Devenport, J. L., Stinson, V., Cutler, B. L., & Kravitz, D. A. (2002). How effective are the expert testimony and cross-examination safeguards? Jurors' perceptions of the suggestiveness and fairness of biased lineup procedures. *Journal of Applied Psychology, 87*, 1042–1054.

Doob, A. N., & Kirshenbaum, H. M. (1973). Bias in police lineups ± partial remembering. *Journal of Police Science and Administration, 1*, 287–293.

Douglass, A. B., & Steblay, N. (2006). Memory distortion in eyewitnesses: A meta-analysis of the post-identification feedback effect. *Applied Cognitive Psychology, 20*, 859–869.

Dunning, D., & Perretta, S. (2002). Automaticity and eyewitness accuracy: A 10- to 12-second rule for distinguishing accurate from inaccurate positive identifications. *Journal of Applied Psychology, 87*, 951–962.

Dysart, J. E. (2008). Alcohol intoxication, impact on eyewitness memory. In B. L. Cutler (Ed.), *Encyclopedia of psychology and law* (pp. 11–13). Thousand Oaks, CA: Sage Publications.

Dysart, J. E., Lindsay, R. C. L., MacDonald, T. K., & Wicke, C. (2002). The intoxicated witness: Effects of alcohol on identification accuracy from showups. *Journal of Applied Psychology, 87,* 170–175.

Faigman, D. L. (2008). Expert testimony, qualifications of experts. In B. L. Cutler (Ed.), *Encyclopedia of psychology and law* (pp. 280–282). Thousand Oaks, CA: Sage Publications.

Federal Rules of Evidence for United States Courts and Magistrates (1975). St. Paul, MN: West Publishing Company.

Fisher, R. P., & Cutler, B. L. (1996). The relation between consistency and accuracy of eyewitness testimony. In G. M. Davies, S. Lloyd-Bostock, M. McMurran, & C. Wilson (Eds.), *Psychology and law: Advances in research* (pp. 21–28). Berlin: De Gruyter.

Frank, J., & Frank, B. (1957). *Not guilty.* London: Gallanez.

Garrett, B. (2008). Judging innocence. *Columbia Law Review, 108,* 55–142.

Garrioch, L., & Brimacombe, C. A. E. (2001). Lineup administrators' expectations: Their impact on eyewitness confidence. *Law and Human Behavior, 25,* 299–315.

Gorenstein, G. W., & Ellsworth, P. C. (1980). Effect of choosing an incorrect photograph on a later identification by an eyewitness. *Journal of Applied Psychology, 5,* 616–622.

Greathouse, S. M., & Kovera, M. B. (2009). Instruction bias and lineup presentation moderate the effects of administrator knowledge on eyewitness identification. *Law and Human Behavior, 33,* 70–82.

Haw, R. M., & Fisher, R. P. (2004). Effects of administrator–witness contact on eyewitness identification accuracy. *Journal of Applied Psychology, 89,* 1106–1112.

Huff, C. R. (1987). Wrongful conviction: Societal tolerance of injustice. *Research in Social Problems and Public Policy, 4,* 99–115.

International Association of the Chiefs of Police (IACP). (2006). *Training key on eyewitness identification.* Alexandria, VA: International Association of the Chiefs of Police.

Kassin, S. M., Ellsworth, P. C., & Smith, V. L. (1989). The "general acceptance" of psychological research on eyewitness testimony: A survey of the experts. *American Psychologist, 44,* 1089–1098.

Kassin, S. M., Tubb, V. A., Hosch, H. M., & Memon, A. (2001). On the "general acceptance" of eyewitness testimony research. *American Psychologist, 56,* 405–416.

Klobuchar, A., Steblay, N., & Caligiuri, H. (2006). Improving eyewitness identifications: Hennepin County's blind sequential lineup project. *Cardozo Public Law, Policy, and Ethics Journal, 4,* 381–413.

Kovera, M. B., Gresham, A. W., Borgida, E., Gray, E., & Regan, P. C. (1997). Does expert testimony inform or influence juror decision-making? A social cognitive analysis. *Journal of Applied Psychology, 82,* 178–191.

Krafka, C., & Penrod, S. (1985). Reinstatement of context in a field experiment on eyewitness identification. *Journal of Personality and Social Psychology, 49,* 58–69.

Laughery, K. R., Alexander, J. F., & Lane, A. B. (1971). Recognition of human faces: Effects of target exposure time, target position, and type of photograph. *Journal of Applied Psychology, 59,* 490–496.

Leippe, M. R. (1995). The case for expert testimony about eyewitness memory. *Psychology, Public Policy, and Law, 1,* 909–959.

Leippe, M. R., Eisenstadt, D., Rauch, S. M., & Seib, H. (2004). Timing of eyewitness expert testimony, jurors' need for cognition, and case strength as determinants of trial verdicts. *Journal of Applied Psychology, 89,* 524–541.

Li, J. C., Dunning, D., & Malpass, R. S. (1998, March). *Cross-racial identification among European-Americans: Basketball fandom and the contact hypothesis.* Paper presented at the biennial meeting of the American Psychology-Law Society, Redondo Beach, CA.

Lindsay, R. C. L., Ross, D. F., Read, J. D., & Toglia, M. P. (Eds.), *Handbook of eyewitness testimony.* (Volumes I & II). Mahwah, NJ: Erlbaum.

Lindsay, R. C. L., & Wells, G. L. (1985). Improving eyewitness identification from lineups: Simultaneous versus sequential lineup presentations. *Journal of Applied Psychology, 70,* 556–564.

Lindsay, R. C. L., Wells, G. L., & O'Connor, F. (1989). Mock juror belief of accurate and inaccurate eyewitnesses: A replication. *Law and Human Behavior, 13,* 333–340.

Loftus, E. F., Loftus, G. R., & Messo, J. (1987). Some facts about "weapon focus." *Law & Human Behavior, 11*(1), 55–62.

Luus, C. A. E., & Wells, G. L. (1994). The malleability of eyewitness confidence: Co-witness and perseverance effects. *Journal of Applied Psychology, 79,* 714–723.

Malpass, R. S., & Devine, P. G. (1981). Eyewitness identification: Lineup instructions and the absence of the offender. *Journal of Applied Psychology, 66,* 482–489.

Malpass, R. S., Tredoux, C. G., & McQuiston-Surrett, D. (2007). Lineup construction and fairness. In R. C. Lindsay, D. F. Ross, J. D. Read, & M. P. Toglia (Eds.), *The handbook of eyewitness psychology, Vol II: Memory for people* (pp. 155–178). Mahwah, NJ: Lawrence Erlbaum Associates Publishers.

McQuiston-Surrett, D. E., Malpass, R. S., & Tredoux, C. G. (2006). Sequential vs. simultaneous lineups: A review of methods, data, and theory. *Psychology, Public Policy and Law, 12,* 137–169.

Mecklenburg, S. H. (2006). *Report to the legislature of the State of Illinois: The Illinois pilot program on sequential double-blind lineup procedures.* Retrieved June 10, 2008, from http://www.chicagopolice.org/IL%20Pilot%20on%20Eyewitness%20ID.pdf.

Meissner, C. A., & Brigham, J. C. (2001). Thirty years of investigating the own-race bias in memory for faces: A meta-analytic review. *Psychology, Public Policy, and Law, 7*, 3–35.

Memon, A., Hope, L., Bartlett, J., & Bull, R. H. C. (2002). Eyewitness recognition errors: The effects of mugshot viewing and choosing in young and old adults. *Memory & Cognition, 30*, 1219–1227.

Memon, A., Hope, L., & Bull, R. (2003). Exposure duration: Effects on eyewitness accuracy and confidence. *British Journal of Psychology, 94*, 339–354.

Monahan, J., & Walker, L. (1986). Social authority: Obtaining, evaluating, and establishing social science in law. *University of Pennsylvania Law Review, 134*, 477–517.

Morgan, C. A., III, Hazlett, G., Doran, A., Garrett, S., Hoyt, G., Thomas, P., et al. (2004). Accuracy of eyewitness memory for persons encountered during exposure to highly intense stress. *International Journal of the Law and Psychiatry, 27*, 265–279.

Ng, W., & Lindsay, R. C. L. (1994). Cross-race facial recognition. *Journal of Cross-Cultural Psychology, 2*, 217–232.

O'Rourke, T. E., Penrod, S. D., Cutler, B. L., & Stuve, T. E. (1989). The external validity of eyewitness identification research: Generalizing across subject populations. *Law and Human Behavior, 13*, 385–395.

Phillips, M. R., McAuliff, B. D., Kovera, M. B., & Cutler, B. L. (1999). Double-blind photoarray administration as a safeguard against investigator bias. *Journal of Applied Psychology, 84*(6), 940–951.

Pickel, K. L. (1998). Unusualness and threat as possible causes of "weapon focus." *Memory, 6*, 277–295.

Pickel, K. L. (1999). The influence of context on the "weapon focus" effect. *Law and Human Behavior, 23*(3), 299–311.

Pigott, M. A., Brigham, J. C., & Bothwell, R. K. (1990). A field study of the relationship between quality of eyewitnesses' descriptions and identification accuracy. *Journal of Police Science and Administration, 17*, 84–88.

Platz, S. J., & Hosch, H. M. (1988). Cross-racial/ethnic eyewitness identification: A field study. *Journal of Applied Social Psychology, 18*, 972–984.

Read, J. D. (1995). The availability heuristic in person identification: The sometimes misleading consequences of enhanced contextual information. *Applied Cognitive Psychology, 9*, 91–122.

Read, J. D., Tollestrup, P., Hammersley, R., McFadzen, E., & Christensen, A. (1990). The unconscious transference effect: Are innocent bystanders ever misidentified? *Applied Cognitive Psychology, 4*, 3–31.

Read, J. D., Yuille, J. C., & Tollestrup, P. (1992). Recollections of a robbery: Effects of arousal and alcohol upon recall and person identification. *Law and Human Behavior, 16*, 425–446.

Rosenthal, R. (1976). *Experimenter effects in behavioral research*. New York: Irvington Publishers.

Ross, S. J., & Malpass, R. M. (2008). Moving forward: Responses to "studying eyewitness investigations in the field". *Law and Human Behavior, 32,* 16–21.

Ross, D. F., Marsil, D., & Metzger, R. (2008). Unconscious transference and mistaken identity: Factor or fiction? In B. L. Cutler (Ed.), *Encyclopedia of psychology and law* (pp. 821–822). Thousand Oaks, CA: Sage Publications.

Russano, M. B., Dickinson, J. J., Greathouse, S. M., & Kovera, M. B. (2006). "Why don't you take another look at number three?" Investigator knowledge and its effects on eyewitness confidence and identification decisions. *Cardozo Public Law, Policy, and Ethics Journal, 4,* 355–379.

Schacter, D., Dawes, R., Jacoby, L. L., Kahneman, D., Lempert, R., Roediger, H. L., et al. (2008). Policy forum: Studying eyewitness investigations in the field. *Law and Human Behavior, 32,* 3–5.

Schmechel, R. S., O'Toole, T. P., Easterly, C., & Loftus, E. F. (2006). Beyond the ken: Testing juror's understanding of eyewitness reliability evidence. *Jurimetrics, 46,* 177–214.

Shadish, W. R., Cook, T. D., & Campbell, D. T. (2002). *Experimental and quasi-experimental designs for generalized causal inference.* New York: Houghton Mifflin.

Shapiro, P., & Penrod, S. D. (1986). A meta-analysis of the facial identification literature. *Psychological Bulletin, 100,* 139–156.

Sporer, S. L., Penrod, S., Read, D., & Cutler, B. (1995). Choosing, confidence, and accuracy: A meta-analysis of the confidence–accuracy relation in eyewitness identification studies. *Psychological Bulletin, 118,* 315–327.

Steblay, N. K. (2008). Commentary on "Studying eyewitness investigations in the field": A look forward. *Law and Human Behavior, 32,* 11–15.

Steblay, N. M. (1997). Social influences in eyewitness recall: A meta-analytic review of lineup instruction effects. *Law & Human Behavior, 21,* 283–297.

Steblay, N. M. (1992). A meta-analytic review of the weapon focus effect. *Law and Human Behavior, 16,* 413–424.

Steblay, N. M., Dysart, J., Fulero, S., & Lindsay, R. C. L. (2001). Eyewitness accuracy rates in sequential and simultaneous line-up presentations: A meta-analytic comparison. *Law and Human Behavior, 25,* 459–474.

Steblay, N. M., Dysart, J., Fulero, S., & Lindsay, R. C. L. (2003). Eyewitness accuracy rates in police showup and lineup presentations: A meta-analytic comparison. *Law and Human Behavior, 27,* 523–540.

Steele, C. M., & Josephs, R. A. (1990). Alcohol myopia: Its prized and dangerous effects. *American Psychologist, 45,* 921–933.

Stinson, V., Devenport, J. L., Cutler, B. L., & Kravitz, D. A. (1996). How effective is the presence-of-counsel safeguard? Attorney perceptions of suggestiveness, fairness, and correctability of biased lineup procedures. *Journal of Applied Psychology, 81,* 64–75.

Stinson, V., Devenport, J. L., Cutler, B. L., & Kravitz, D. A. (1997). How effective is the motion-to-suppress safeguard? Judges' perceptions of suggestiveness and fairness of biased lineup procedures. *Journal of Applied Psychology, 82,* 211–220.

Susa, K. J., & Meissner, C. A. (2008). Eyewitness descriptions, accuracy of. In B. L. Cutler (Ed.), *Encyclopedia of psychology and law* (pp. 285–287). Thousand Oaks, CA: Sage Publications.

Technical Working Group on Eyewitness Evidence. (1999). *Eyewitness evidence: A guide for law enforcement.* Washington, DC: U.S. Department of Justice.

Tollestrup, P., Turtle, J., & Yuille, J. (1994). Actual victims and witnesses to robbery and fraud: An archival analysis. In D. F. Ross, J. D. Read, & M. P. Toglia (Eds.), *Adult eyewitness testimony: Current trends and developments* (pp. 144–160). New York, NY: Cambridge University Press.

Tredoux, C. G. (1998). Statistical inference on measures of lineup fairness. *Law and Human Behavior, 22,* 217–237.

Valentine, T., & Heaton, P. (1999). An evaluation of the fairness of police line-ups and video identifications. *Applied Cognitive Psychology, 13,* S59–S72.

Valentine, T., Pickering, A., & Darling, S. (2003). Characteristics of eyewitness identifications that predict the outcome of real lineups. *Applied Cognitive Psychology, 17,* 969–993.

Van Wallendael, L. R., Devenport, J. L., Cutler, B. L., & Penrod, S. D. (2007). Mistaken identification = erroneous convictions? Assessing and improving legal safeguards. In R. C. L. Lindsay, D. F. Ross, J. D. Read, & M. P. Toglia (Eds.), *Handbook of eyewitness testimony* (pp. 557–582). Mahwah, NJ: Erlbaum.

Weber, N., Brewer, N., Wells, G. L., Semmler, C., & Keast, A. (2004). Eyewitness identification accuracy and response latency: The unruly 10–12 second rule. *Journal of Experimental Psychology: Applied, 10,* 139–147.

Wells, G. L. (1978). Applied eyewitness testimony research: System variables and estimator variables. *Journal of Personality and Social Psychology, 36,* 1546–1557.

Wells, G. L. (1985). Verbal descriptions of faces from memory: Are they diagnostic of identification accuracy? *Journal of Applied Psychology, 70,* 619–626.

Wells, G. L. (2006). Eyewitness identification: Systemic reforms. *Wisconsin Law Review, 2006,* 615–643.

Wells, G. L. (2008). Field experiments on eyewitness identification: Towards a better understanding of pitfalls and prospects. *Law and Human Behavior, 32,* 6–10.

Wells, G. L., & Bradfield, A. L. (1999). Measuring the goodness of lineups: Parameter estimation, question effects, and limits to the mock witness paradigm. *Applied Cognitive Psychology, 13*, S27–S39.

Wells, G. L., Leippe, M. R., & Ostrom, T. M. (1979). Guidelines for empirically assessing the fairness of a lineup. *Law and Human Behavior, 3*, 285–293.

Wells, G. L., Malpass, R. S., Lindsay, R. C. L., Fisher, R. P., Turtle, J. W., & Fulero, S. M. (2000). From the lab to the police station: A successful application of eyewitness research. *American Psychologist, 55*, 581–598.

Wells, G. L., Rydell, S. M., & Seelau, E. P. (1993). On the selection of distracters for eyewitness lineups. *Journal of Applied Psychology, 78*, 835–844.

Wells, G. L., Small, M., Penrod, S., Malpass, R. S., Fulero, S. M., & Brimacombe, C. A. E. (1998). Eyewitness identification procedures: Recommendations for lineups and photospreads. *Law and Human Behavior, 22*, 603–646.

Wogalter, M. S., Malpass, R. S., & McQuiston, D. E. (2004). A national survey of police on preparation and conduct of identification lineups. *Psychology, Crime and Law, 10*, 69–82.

Wright, D. B., & McDaid, A. T. (1996). Comparing system and estimator variables using data from real line-ups. *Applied Cognitive Psychology, 10*, 75–84.

Wright, D. B., & Skagerberg, E. M. (2007). Post-identification feedback affects real eyewitnesses. *Psychological Science, 18*, 172–178.

Yarmey, A. D., Yarmey, M. J., & Yarmey, A. L. (2006). Accuracy of eyewitness identifications in showups and lineups. *Law and Human Behavior, 20*, 459–477.

Cases and Statutes

Daubert v. Merrell Dow Pharmaceuticals, 509 U.S. 579 (1993).

Frye v. United States, 293 F. 1013 (D.C. Cir. 1923).

General Electric Co., et al., v. Joiner et ux., 522 U.S. 136 (1997).

Kumho Tire Company v. Carmichael, 526 U.S. 137 (1999).

Manson v. Braithwaite, 432 U.S. 98, 1977.

Neil v. Biggers, 409 U.S. 188, 1972.

United States v. Telfaire, 1978 469 F.2d 552, 558–59.

Key Terms

archival studies: retrospective studies of eyewitness identification that rely on filed reports.

beyond the ken: the content of expert testimony that is outside the general knowledge of lay persons.

blind administration: the presentation of a photoarray or a lineup to a witness by an investigator who does not know which photo or person is the suspect.

cross-examination: testimony provided in response to questioning by the attorney who did not call the witness; more likely to take on an adversarial tone.

direct examination: testimony provided in response to questioning by the attorney who called the witness; more likely to be conducted in a supportive tone.

***Daubert* test:** a legal test for the admissibility of scientific evidence in which the judge rules on whether the evidence is admissible, using criteria that may include whether the scientific basis for the evidence (a) has been tested or is testable, (b) has been peer reviewed, (c) has an acceptable error rate, and (d) is generally accepted in the field.

erroneous conviction: conviction of a person charged with a crime he did not commit.

estimator variables: conditions that are outside the control of investigators but are known to influence the accuracy of eyewitness identification.

expert testimony about the psychology of eyewitness memory: the testimony by a person (usually a cognitive or social psychologist) knowledgeable about memory processes and the factors known from research to influence eyewitness identification accuracy.

eyewitness testimony: the testimony given to investigators or in a court by victims or bystanders to crime.

field studies : studies of eyewitness identification conducted in naturalistic settings, such as actual criminal investigations or simulated crimes in the community.

fillers: persons or photographs of persons known to be innocent but selected for inclusion in a live lineup or a photoarray.

Frye **test:** a legal standard for admissibility of scientific or expert evidence, using "general acceptance in the field" as the criterion for whether the basis of the evidence is acceptable.

general acceptance: the extent to which experts in the relevant scientific field agree about a particular phenomenon and the factors that influence it.

general impairment factors: conditions surrounding the crime that reduce the accuracy of eyewitness identifications.

guiding discovery: providing input into the process of investigating a case.

hindsight bias: the research finding that people overestimate the predictability of events when they know that the events have already occurred.

identification tests: techniques that rely on person recognition by eyewitnesses and designed to test whether a suspect is a crime perpetrator.

initial consultation: the preliminary discussions that occur between an attorney and an expert concerning the possible retainer of an expert in the case.

juror confusion: the extent to which jurors misunderstand or as a result of misunderstanding misapply expert testimony.

live lineups: a suspect and a set of fillers presented live to an eyewitness as part of an identification test.

meta-analysis: a research methodology for statistically combining the results of multiple studies to derive general conclusions about a body of research literature.

mistaken identification: the erroneous identification of an innocent person as a crime perpetrator.

mugshots: photos of suspects shown to an eyewitness usually at the early stages of investigations in order to obtain leads in a case.

mugshot commitment effect: The research finding that identification of a suspect from one identification test (e.g., selecting a suspect's mugshot early in an investigation) increases the likelihood that the same suspect will be identified from subsequent identification tests (e.g., identifying the same suspect from a photoarray later in an investigation).

nonblind administration: the presentation of a photoarray or lineup to a witness by an investigator who knows which photo or person is the suspect.

own-race bias: the research finding that people are more accurate at identifying members of their own race than members of other races and make more mistakes when identifying members of other races than when identifying members of their own race.

perpetrator-absent lineups: lineups in which the crime perpetrator is not present; instead the suspect is innocent.

perpetrator-description-matched fillers: fillers chosen for a lineup or a photoarray based on their resemblance to the witness's description of the crime perpetrator.

perpetrator-present lineups: lineups that contain the crime perpetrator as a suspect.

photoarrays: sets of photographs containing a suspect and fillers (known innocents) used in an identification test.

postdictors of identification accuracy: aspects of the witness's testimony, such as confidence and consistency, that are believed (sometimes mistakenly) to predict the accuracy of eyewitness identification.

prejudicial impact versus probative value: the weighing of an expert's potential to mislead or bias a jury against the assistance that the testimony provides to the jury.

prospective studies: studies of eyewitness identification that rely on the collection of data from future simulations or crimes.

random assignment: the allocation of research participants to experimental conditions in such a manner that each participant has an equal likelihood of being allocated to each experimental condition.

re-direct examination: testimony provided in response to questioning by the attorney who called the witness, following cross-examination, with the purpose of addressing issues that arose during cross-examination.

retention interval: the amount of time that passes between the crime and the identification.

sequestration rule: designed to prevent collusion and fabrication of testimony, this rule requires witnesses to be separated and to not hear one another's testimony.

showups: the presentation of a single suspect to an eyewitness for identification, usually at or near the scene or crime and shortly after the crime occurs.

suspect bias factors: conditions of identification tests that either increase the likelihood of identifications of suspects (whether innocent or guilty) or make it difficult to determine whether an identification is the product of a witness's memory of a perpetrator or other factors, such as guessing, deduction, or social influence.

suspect-matched fillers: fillers chosen for a lineup or a photoarray based on their resemblance to the suspect.

systematic manipulation of variables: a feature of experimental psychology research wherein the investigator holds certain factors constant while causing others to vary according to a planned schedule.

unconscious transference: the mistaking of an innocent person for a crime perpetrator based on familiarity with the innocent person from another context (with the witness not realizing that the person is familiar from another context).

voir dire: the process by which individuals from a jury pool are selected to serve on a jury for a specific case.

weapon focus effect: the research finding that the visual presence of a weapon draws an eyewitness's attention from the perpetrator to the weapon and thereby impairs subsequent identification accuracy.

Index

Note: Page Numbers followed by *f* denotes Figures and *t* denotes Tables.

About the Authors

Brian Cutler, PhD, is a professor at the University of Ontario Institute of Technology. He is a fellow of the Association for Psychological Science and Distinguished Member of the American Psychology-Law Society (APLS). Cutler has received several National Science Foundation (NSF) grants for his research on eyewitness identification and has authored or coauthored more than 80 books, book chapters, and refereed journal articles. Cutler is Editor-in-Chief of *Law and Human Behavior*, the flagship *Psychology and Law* journal, and has recently edited the *Encyclopedia of Psychology and Law*. In addition, Cutler has served as consultant and expert witness in over 100 cases in various U.S. state and federal courts.

Margaret Bull Kovera, PhD, is Professor of Psychology at John Jay College of Criminal Justice, City University of New York. She is a fellow of the American Psychological Association, the American Psychology-Law Society (APLS), and the Society for the Psychological Study of Social Issues and is the past president of APLS. She has received the Saleem Shah Award for Early Career Achievement in Psychology and Law and the APLS Outstanding Teacher and Mentor in Psychology and Law Award from APLS. Her research has been published in *Law and Human Behavior*, *Journal of Applied Psychology*, *Applied Cognitive Psychology*, and *Psychology, Public Policy, and Law*. For over a decade, she has had continuous funding from the National Science Foundation for her research on eyewitness identification and jury decision making. She regularly serves as a consultant and expert witness in cases involving eyewitness identification.